SHARKS and SHIPWRECKS

HUGH EDWARDS

A Demeter Press Book
Quadrangle/The New York Times Book Co.

SHARKS and SHIPWRECKS

For Marilyn and Christopher

Library of Congress Catalog Card Number:
74-33219

International Standard Book Number:
0-8129-0559-8

Printed in the United States of America

Third printing, April 1976

Contents

Preface

The sea, with its changing moods and mysterious deeps, has always fascinated men. Legends of lost ships, drowned treasures, mermaids, sea serpents, and the sound of the church bells of sunken cities, are part of our earliest folk lore.

The fish of the sea have been a bounty for men since earliest times, and we have used it as a high road for our ships for three thousand years. But men have never really understood the sea, though they may have loved it, feared it, or hated it, in a complex of contradictory emotions as the poets tell us.

For Kipling it was 'The old grey widow maker'. Robert Browning told of 'The Hell of waters where they howl and hiss . . .' But for John Masefield it was a compulsion. 'I must go down to the sea again, to the lonely sea and the sky!'

Through it all the sea remains unmoved and unconquered. It is one of the ironic facts of our own age that though men have walked on the Moon and circled Mars with their rockets, they have yet to reach the bottom of the deep oceans on our own planet.

The ocean remains a challenge. The last frontier of exploration.

This book is about the challenge. About divers, men and women, who know the sea as well as anyone. Each tells their own story of triumph or tragedy according to their particular circumstances. The chapters are of sharks, shipwrecks ancient and modern, of treasure, and the courage of men under stress and pain so severe they hardly comprehend what is happening to them. As a balance there is the search for beauty below the silver skin of the surface, and the quest for knowledge.

Each story is different, for divers are individualists. But in an ever-changing world there are two constants. The sea and the human spirit.

The divers in these pages are Australians and New Zealanders. But they could be from any country. For the human spirit is wider than national borders, and the sea itself knows no boundaries.

Hugh Edwards 1974

Filming
the
Great White Shark

RON TAYLOR

The great white shark, *Carcharodon carcharias*, Old Rough Teeth, and cameraman Ron Taylor have met eye-to-eye, tooth-to-lens, on a number of occasions.

A former world spearfishing champion, Taylor now shoots fish and sharks only with a camera. He has won numerous photographic awards, including the International Underwater Film Festival at Santa Monica, U.S.A., a Premio Sarra prize, the British Portfolio Award, and Portuguese International Salon gold medals, and world-wide recognition for his work.

American Peter Gimbel who made the underwater film of the decade, *Blue Water White Death*, released in 1972, describes Ron simply as 'by far the best diver I've ever worked with. Superb in his preparations for a dive, sound in his knowledge, quick to detect a flaw and ingenious in solving problems.' Gimbel adds, 'He is a real pro who retains the enthusiasm of an amateur—which I reckon is about the highest praise you can hand a professional.'

In 1969, Gimbel had followed reports of sightings of white sharks through the Indian Ocean from Durban to Malagasy and Shri Lanka in a hired ex-whale chaser, the *Terrier*, at extraordinary expense without sighting even a retreating fin.

In January 1970, on Taylor's advice, Gimbel—who had already spent a fortune on the film—made one last throw of the dice. He took his film crew, including Taylor, to Spencer Gulf in South Australia, on an expedition gamble which would make or break his film.

In the submerged cages hanging off our mother ship *Saori* we watched and waited by Dangerous Reef, tensed and poised behind our cameras, straining our eyes for the movement of pale torpedo shapes out beyond the twilight limit of underwater visibility.

The tension was electric. I could see it in the stance of the Americans in their cage, waiting too. They had come half-way round the world for this, to Spencer Gulf in South Australia, and already we had been unsuccessful a depressingly longer period than we had expected.

Would the sharks we had seen from the surface come in? Would we get film? Or would they be spooked by the cages, and the project remain as cursed and unlucky as it had in the previous year . . .

I hoped for Peter's sake the sharks would come in. He deserved some luck, a break, a reward for persistence, faith, and—yes, courage.

There was a movement beyond visibility, a glimpse of something huge moving in the distance. Then with almost disconcerting suddenness the first white shark appeared with leisurely strokes of its tail.

'Here he comes!' I said to myself, feeling a surge of gratitude and relief. Snuggling the big Arriflex camera in its black case tight in to my shoulder, I looked along the sights waiting for the moment.

I pressed the trigger and kept the camera rolling on. The shark swerved arrogantly in, past the two cages, looking at us with the dark eyes that seemed more like black holes in its head from a distance.

But there was nothing ugly about him. He appeared magnificent, moving with unhurried yet efficient speed. Conical snout, mouth slightly open to show the splayed lower teeth. Balanced on his pectoral fins, and every inch a hunting, prowling predator.

I could hear the other cameras going and knew what the Americans, Peter Gimbel and Stan Waterman, would be thinking. These few minutes (we hoped they would be hours) in the cages with the white sharks in frame and focus had cost hundreds of thousands of dollars. A communion with the world's rarest and most dangerous shark. The great white. Also called the white pointer or white death.

The shark turned. Three metres from the cage he wrinkled his nose, bared his teeth and opened his mouth wide. I could see the attack pattern forming and gripped my camera tight.

Without slackening speed he swam straight up to the cage. There was a momentary glimpse of a white palisade of fangs and beyond them the red tunnel of his gullet—a sight usually only seen by creatures about to die.

Then he hit the top float of the cage without slackening speed. If it had been a seal the sharp dagger teeth with the momentum of more than 450 kg of shark behind them would have inflicted a terrible tearing, shearing wound. Instead there was just the sickening scrunch of ivory on metal over the sound of our cameras.

The shark recoiled and shook his head like a boxer who has taken a sharp left hook. 'Is he spooked?' I wondered. 'Is this the end of it?'

But the shark was far from discouraged. He came back to mouth the bars all the way down the cage with a screech of teeth on metal which sent shivers up the back of our wet suits.

Less than arm's length from the great conical snout and teeth working on the bars, I found myself looking into the huge dark eye, and wondered what was turning in the brain behind the bullet nose of the beast.

'What are you thinking shark, about the funny creatures behind the bars, and the smell of the blood and baits in the water? Would you eat us if you could get at us?'

As he rolled past, the eye of the shark—the boldest of the three we had seen from the surface—remained fixed on us. Like a dog outside a chicken coop.

'Hope the cage holds', I thought. It was none-too-robust, and a detached part of my mind wondered what we would do if he forced his way through the bars. 'Bang him on the nose with a camera, I suppose and bail out quick', I answered myself. But it wasn't a very convincing thought. The shark would get to us if he wanted to, before we reached the boat.

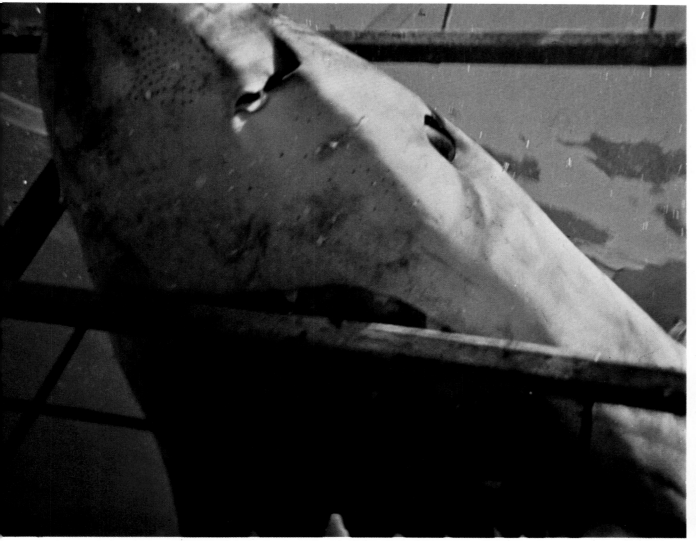

Also I knew from experience that nothing would turn away a determined white on his first attack run except death itself.

'There he goes!' The shark half-rolled, slammed the cage contemptuously with his tail, and disappeared under *Saori*'s keel.

I looked automatically at the film counter on the camera to see how much footage I had left, then turned and grinned at the other cameramen in the other cage. They gave me a signal of pure delight. Triumph at last. The fact we had waited so many frustrated months made it all the sweeter.

Then the shark was back.

The same one? No, it was another, and this one too went through the same routine. First they attacked the cages while our cameras ran steadily, then they finned away to tug and rend at the horse meat baits hanging from the ship and the corners of the cages.

The pattern was continuous and just what we wanted. It was better than we had dared hope. Attack, attack, attack. The difference between the whites and other sharks—the whalers and tigers we knew so well—was that while the others could be coaxed into biting at baits, the whites once aroused by blood in the water struck at anything.

They went from the baits to the cage, *Soari*'s keel, the anchor chain, the skiff, even the rudder and propellor. Without viciousness or malice, but calmly and as though driven by an implacable need, they mouthed and bit remorselessly at anything they saw. They maintained the same effortless pace the whole time, never slowing or hurrying.

It was this sinister calm that was in a way the most frightening thing about them. Also the fact that they watched us all the time in the cage, noting our every movement with their great dark eyes, restlessly swimming to and fro, never pausing.

'Pale heavy bodies, with eyes black as holes in a shroud, and slack smiling mouths.' That was the way Peter Matthiessen described them in his excellent book of the film *Blue Meridian*.

And they were frightening. You never became blasé or entirely used to them. Even though we were absorbed in the technical side of our work—getting this remarkable and rarest of all shark scenes on camera—the personalities of the white sharks cut through to our consciousness like a slash from one of those serrated-edged teeth.

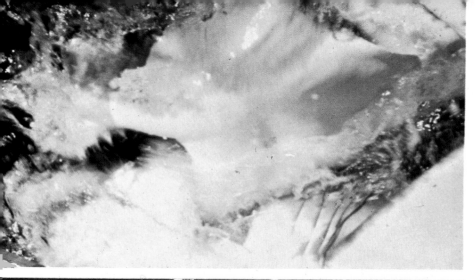

White shark tangled and helpless in cage tether line. ◄

A white pointer attacking and gorging on its hooked comrade. ▲

Often I found the hair prickling on the back of my neck as a shark mouthed the cage. And when the shark looked at me with his dark eye I felt as though he was drawing my soul out through the bars of the cage.

'Empty and impenetrable as the Eye of God', Peter had said. I did not find it entirely so. My own feeling was that there was a strong intelligent personality behind the black orb. Not evil, but more alien and sinister than that.

Whatever it was, we kept in the cages.

Off Durban with the whaling fleet in the Indian Ocean, during the making of Peter Gimbel's film in the previous year, we had swum freely out of the cages among a pack of perhaps 200 oceanic whalers and blue sharks, big sharks all of them, chewing and hacking at the bloody sides of a harpooned sperm whale in a classic feeding frenzy. Probably people would never have believed our story if we hadn't filmed it, because it was thought, (and I would have believed myself) that swimming with large sharks in a feeding frenzy would be certain death. True, the whalers made passes at us, and nuzzled and bumped us, but we held them off with short lengths of stick, rapping their snouts and backs with sharp blows, and felt anxious and occasionally not quite in control of the situation.

At one stage Peter Gimbel swam right up with his wide lens Arriflex camera among the blood and gore, into the huge wound in the sperm whale's belly where the sharks were feeding. He filmed their working mouths from a metre away as they ripped and tore at the flesh. It was an astonishing and incredible scene.

Peter's plan was to have two men constantly filming while two others 'rode shotgun', hitting and jabbing and swatting at the sharks with the billy-sticks as they came near. Peter's theory was as follows. 'The whalers and blues are, in the main, requiems, or scavenger sharks, feeding off dead or sick things. They test by nudge and bump. I am convinced that if they did not get a strong reaction after a bump they would bite. Therefore we had to react strongly, pushing them, or clubbing them, but never staying still or failing to react aggressively.'

It was a weird scene out there alongside our South African mother ship, the *Terrier*, a dead whale lashed alongside her, and three kilometres of blue-black ocean under us. We had rubber dinghies on top, the cages as refuges, and sharks, sharks, and sharks, gnawing and tearing at the whale.

It seemed that the sharks accepted us as ancillary scavengers also attracted

13

Huge white swimming past Ron in cage.

by the whale—like pilot fish, and remoras, and jacks and king fish, and the great heavy albatrosses and petrels which tore at the carcase with sharp beaks on the surface. They were also unmolested.

The white sharks were quite different. There was never any question that they were the dominant force in the waters off Dangerous Reef. As long as they were nosing around the baits no other sharks, rays, or other fish, were in sight.

After the first day's shooting, when we had that wonderful knowledge that we had positive good film of whites in the can, we naturally considered how to improve it on successive days. We talked in our evening conferences about swimming with them. I felt that one white could probably be handled alright, but more than one could be dangerous, particularly in the bad cold water visibility.

With any sharks a diver relies on bluff—the psychological advantage. The oceanic whaler sharks off South Africa had the strength and equipment to kill us if they had wanted to—human beings with main arteries below the soft skins of arms and legs are very vulnerable to shark attack.

The white shark is much more formidably equipped than the whaler, with a huge mouth, and terrible shearing teeth. Triangular shaped with serrations on each side, like a steak knife, and up to fifty millimetres long and twenty-five millimetres wide in big specimens. But it is not the white's physical equipment which is as impressive as his attitude.

The white has an entirely different personality. He has no sense of fear, and is absolutely confident. Therefore he cannot be bluffed. If he is hungry he bites —anything.

Even though he may not actually eat a human the bite could well be fatal. I have friends among divers who survived white shark attacks. Henri Bource who lost a leg off Lady Julia Percy Island in Victoria, Brian Rodger and Rodney Fox in South Australia. The injuries, from attacks which were not pressed home to the limit, were frightful. They were all quite remarkably lucky inasmuch as they were got to hospital and skilled medical treatment within one and a half hours of the attack. Normally it would take much longer. If it had taken three hours any of the three would have been dead. Others, like young Geoffrey Corner in South Australia, did die. Usually from massive blood loss.

Many of the shark attacks, and most of the fatal ones, on divers around the world have been by white sharks. Perhaps they mistake the black wet suits and flippers for seals—who knows? I think myself that a hungry white would attack any large prey.

At any rate we did not solve the problem of swimming in open water to film them. It is true that we could probably have killed one with an explosive-headed spear, a power-head, if it attacked.

But our purpose was to film live sharks not dead ones. There has been too much of that. And at Dangerous Reef we knew we couldn't bluff the big whites. Rather they had the psychological call over *us*. We were sure they would bite at us and, unlike *Saori*'s massive wooden rudder, or the outboard motor, they would probably do us a lot of damage.

As it was there were some hairy moments.

We knew that the aluminium cages—built light for easy handling in the water —would not withstand a really determined attack by a great white. There was always a slightly heart-in-mouth feeling when one chewed the bars or slammed into the cage that this might be IT—the time a white really did get to a cameraman.

Of course the danger made better film of it.

Like the time Peter Lake was in a cage getting still camera shots with a 180 degree fish-eye lens. A huge white shark about four metres long, got tangled in a cage bait line and in its thrashing to get free stretched and bent five of the bars. The tumbled and unhappy Lake inside thought the cage was going to disintegrate completely. 'Boy!' he said afterwards, 'When I saw those bars starting to go I felt like I had jumped at 12,000 ft with my parachute eaten by rats!'

However, he kept cool and did what he couldn't have done in a parachute. He reached down and got out his leg knife, and cut the shark free.

Valerie, my wife, and I had a similar experience on a different occasion. The whites were very prone to tangling in the bait and tether lines. This time the cage was getting rattled like a cocktail shaker and banging on the boat. In the confusion someone cast off the tether line, and there we were floating round Spencer Gulf tied on to nothing but an enraged great white shark! We got out OK, but it was an exciting moment.

In between swimming the cages, the whites attacked the baits hung from the ship's rail, and gave some dramatic surface demonstrations of their attacking technique to the people on board. The biggest shark of the days we filmed, a shark over four metres, surged out of the water one day to drag down a quarter of dead horse hanging in the air from a davit. It stood right out of the water held up by a beating tail, head and gills clear and black eye rolling white, to grab the horse flesh, tear it loose with massive shakes of its head and drag it to the bottom.

The watchers saw, with chilled stomachs, how death could come to a careless seal on the rocks, or a man on a life-raft . . .

The white can have few enemies. They are so big and so powerful that probably only the killer whale or sperm whale would be any kind of threat. The main danger to a white is another white—or man.

I have often wondered what goes on in the minds of the great sharks in their kill-or-be-killed twilight world of the great oceans.

I know that there are bigger whites than the ones we filmed at Dangerous Reef. Those were all males, and it is well known that the females grow much bigger.

One of the problems with making films, and especially films about sharks, is that you always have to do something different or better than the last time.

Against this you have the difficulty that, with the expansion of human activities, pollution, fishing, and so on, sharks suitable for photography are becoming increasingly hard to find.

Peter Gimbel gambled, and spent a fortune of investment money to make his film. We were lucky (though we worked hard as well) and it more than paid off. It was a truly magnificent film.

I can't imagine doing anything better. But the mind keeps turning with ideas and schemes, and possibilities, coming to the surface all the time.

We will be doing more work on white sharks. I'm not sure just how or what we'll do. But we'll be doing it.

After all, there *is* only one white shark. The most spectacular, magnificent, and mightiest of all the sharks in the ocean. The ultimate shark.

The Pieces-of-Eight

HUGH EDWARDS

The *Vergulde Draeck* is one of the great and legendary treasure ships of the Western Australian coast. Wrecked in 1656 with a cargo of silver, she was the object of many treasure-hunting expeditions through the years—beginning with the Dutch themselves, a short time after her loss.

After World War II self-contained underwater breathing apparatus (SCUBA) added a new dimension. But the *Draeck* remained elusive. The shifting sandhills ashore and the maze of kelp-grown reefs out to sea held their secret.

By the 1960s sceptics were beginning to question the existence of the wreck. What if it were some plausible plot by pirates? Or perhaps the latitude had been deliberately falsified in the old records to preserve the treasure from pillaging . . .

But the *Draeck* was there. And close to bearings honestly given in the old journals. With more and more divers using the waters it was only a matter of time before someone stumbled across her.

The day was Easter Saturday, 1963. A party of divers found elephant tusks and cylindrical objects they thought might be cannon south of Lancelin. They were cannon. The wreck was the *Vergulde Draeck*. In the party were Graeme Henderson, Alan Robinson, a long-time Dragon searcher, John Cowen, Jim and Alan Henderson.

I was fortunate to be involved in succeeding dives on what was then a virgin seventeenth century treasure wreck. Each dive was momentous, a milestone in our diving experience. And none more so than the sullen, foul-weathered day on which we found the silver.

Five and a half metres down the wreck lay, among the dark caves and shadowy ledges below the foam. Guns and anchors covered by kelp weed and pink, brittle corals.

The waves broke hard across the Dragon Reef, and there was tension in the divers' narrowed eyes and taut jaw muscles as they watched the boil and suck of the backwash among the rocks where the wreck and the silver were. It would not be an easy dive.

The sound of the surf and the wind isolated each man with his thoughts, but you could read the faces. What would be left down there after three centuries? Bones, bottles, and golden chains, like the Armada ships? The 78,600 guilders of shining silver in eight chests she had carried to the bottom with her . . . ?

'The *Vergulde Draeck* . . . The Gilt, the Golden Dragon . . .'

I spoke the name of the old ship softly and the wind blew the words away so that no-one heard them.

At this place, in the darkness, 307 years before, the East Indiaman had been wrecked on her way to the Spice Islands. A lone snaggle-tooth of rock, dark amidst the spume, marked the spot. Here the *Draeck*, over-running her eastward beat from Africa, had struck and perished. The rocks had slashed deep into her timbers, gutting her and spilling cannon, cargo, and the struggling figures of Netherlands men and women across the reef in the darkness—the agony of shipwreck long ago. Instead of the palm-scented ports of Indonesia and the East, and an aromatic cargo of cloves and nutmeg, she had found a green sea grave off the Australian coast, killing all but a handful of her people.

Our boat, an old cray and shark fishing veteran named the *Dorothy*, with blue peeling paint and a yellow number on her bow, seemed to smell the graveyard. She snatched at her anchor chain like a frightened mare, and her mast swung through wide arcs as the steepening swells passed under her keel. This was the waves' first check in all the 8,000 kilometres from Africa and they struck the reef hard in the fury of it.

Dennis Bennetts, the skipper, frowned. He looked out at the line of low black clouds on the horizon and the anchor line twanging taut on top of a swell.

'You'd better get your dive in quick', he said. 'There's more wind coming up, and the weather side of a reef is no place to get caught.'

Maurie Hammond, the underwater cameraman with the fine sensitive face, gripped my elbow.

'Ready?' he asked hoarsely above the wind. I nodded.

'Right when you are', I said with a dry throat, and picked up my fins and lead belt. We were all in rubber wet suits, black, except for Maurie whose was light blue with a black hood and twin stripes down the sleeves and trousers. The camera, a Rollei-Marine in a big green aluminium case, was hanging around his neck on a rubber strap.

'You've got about half an hour I reckon', said Dennis Bennetts, looking at the sky again.

'Should be long enough', said Hammond.

The others were buckling their lead belts and pulling on masks and fins. Looking out at the surf, the dazzling high-flung spray, and the boil of the backwash, I felt the excitement in the pit of my stomach.

George Brenzi and John Cowen bent over the red compressor and it started with a roar and a cloud of oil smoke.

Alan Robinson swung his tank on to his back and buckled the harness, bracing himself against the gunwhale.

'Watch the surges close to the reef', he said to the rest of us, in a matter-of-fact voice. 'The caves run right back underneath. You don't want to get sucked in.'

He bit on his mouthpiece and went over backwards in a practised motion, landing with a heavy splash and disappeared. A stream of air bubbles pulsing to the surface showed where he was breathing down below.

Jim Henderson was next. 'Here goes!' he said, with a tight smile, and after blowing twice on his mouthpiece to clear it, he was gone too. It was our turn.

'Ready, when you are', said Maurie Hammond, unwinding nylon air hose from a reel. I gave him the thumbs-up signal and we went over together. It was a long drop from the *Dorothy*'s rail, and the shock and cold of the sea took my breath away. I kicked hard away from the side of the boat, spurred by the thought of ten tonnes coming down on me off the top of a wave, and sank quickly in a cloud of bubbles.

The bottom came up to meet me. Kelp weed and rock pinnacles with a school of silver drummer circling in and out of the gloom. Large fish with inquisitive eyes and prim, tight mouths.

The water wasn't clear. It was dirty from the autumn gale. Above, the sea was swollen like the face of a woman who has been crying. Below the surface it was fogged with sediment and particles of floating weed. On the bottom, I worked the air bubbles out of my rubber suit and thought how disappointed Hammond would be about the dirty water. There was a bright red starfish on a rock close by. A brief tug on the line and Hammond was beside me.

He grimaced at the sediment in the water and made the cut-throat sign across his throat with his finger meaning 'No good'. With a small motion of disgust, he gestured to me to go on, and went back to the surface. I saw him briefly silhouetted against the foam-streaked silver sky next to the black whale-shadow of the *Dorothy* above.

The fins of the others were already disappearing towards the reef. As the water shallowed the effect of the waves overhead became more marked. They came with the noise of express trains, sending spiracules of foam reaching down from the surface like fingers, and the seaweed flattened with their passing as

In this drowned valley the bodies of 118 of the passengers and crew of the *Vergulde Draeck* rolled in the surges on that April morning in 1656. Ghosts among the seaweed, returned to life perhaps in the pale bodies of the fish which dwell in the caverns.

Inside the Dragon caves, gloomy places with a huge iron gun leaning across the doorway.

though blown down by a high wind. We were cautious at first, clutching hand-fuls of kelp and bracing our bodies against the surge. But we found we could hold against it quite well—even when it threatened to tear our masks and fins off—so long as we were close to the bottom and had a good grip.

'Life as a rock crab', I muttered. 'Ouch!' A barnacle under my hand broke and a sliver of shell ran a neat gash up my middle finger. The blood at five and a half metres trickled out on the current like green smoke—red colours are lost within a man's depth from the surface.

A moment later the cut was forgotten as I became aware that what I was holding on to was not a rock, as I had thought, but a gun.

'A cannon!' Bubbles puffed from my mouthpiece, and my heart thumped. 'A ship's gun!'

It was swollen with corrosion, grown over with tough-stalked kelp weed and barnacles. But the shape was there, unmistakable, and I could feel the knob at the end, the cascabel and the trunnions which had notched in an oaken gun carriage long ago. The muzzle was partly blocked by kelp roots and a hermit crab lived in the hollow. He picked up his shell and scuttled deeper down the barrel at my approach.

The *Draeck* had ploughed her red lion figurehead through many seas.

The guns had travelled further than the ship perhaps. They were precious and expensive items and exchanged around the fleet as ships were laid-up, refitted, unloaded, or pensioned off. They lasted longer than the vessels and in 1656 a strong iron piece of cannon may have seen many seas through the gunports of many ships.

The guns were always fired in a joyous salvo on a home-coming. When the ships crossed the Texel Bar coming into Amsterdam—a thundering cannonade of smoke and gladness—and gratitude, too. For on the Indies voyages after three or four years away a third or more of the people aboard could die of scurvy and shipboard disease. And for the survivors there was the joy of being alive as well as the home-coming itself. Life and love were sweet to the taste, then as now.

One gun, bigger than the rest, leaned against a cave, almost vertical. There was a white halo of foam around its muzzle and a school of small golden fish hung in the cavern entrance and were silhouetted against the blackness of the cave. The surge sucked me towards it.

20

The big waves came overhead with a roar like express trains, and fizzed out in foam and bubbles which crackled in our ears.

'Steady, boy', I said, gripping a cannon butt.

The cave yawned black behind the gun, and I had no desire to be drawn into the vortex of caverns and tunnels on this day of strong swells.

It was sobering to reflect that in this gully had rolled the drowned bodies of the dead men and women of the *Draeck*. One hundred and eighteen of them were sucked below the foam in the darkness when she broke up, two hours before dawn on April 28th, 1656. 'The *Draeck* was immediately burst open and sunk down', it was reported. 'Of the cargo nothing was saved . . .'

Feeling the strength of the sea at that place I could believe it. It was surprising that they had been able to launch the boats at all, and that seventy-five people had reached the mainland five kilometres away to a place of temporary and doubtful refuge.

'A dead man's reef . . .' I thought. Gliding past and peering into cracks and crevices around the anchor, I remembered the lines from Shakespeare's *Tempest*.

> *Full fathom five thy Father lies*
> *Of his bones are coral made.*
> *Those are pearls that were his eyes . . .*

But there were no pearl-eyed skulls or coral-crusted bones among the fronds of seaweed, though a *Draeck* skeleton was found ashore in the sandhills near a box of coins in the 1930s. His silver would not buy bread or water there, nor deflect a native spear. They were dead weight for a dead man.

Only seven of the seventy-five survivors of the wreck escaped the Great South Land, as the Dutch called Australia. Sent for help in the *Draeck*'s pinnace these men made a remarkable 2400-kilometre voyage to Batavia (modern Djakarta), arriving in the last extremities of hunger and thirst—skeletal figures in a little boat feebly waving their news of shipwreck and disaster.

Rescue ships were sent at once. But neither the first nor any of the successive expeditions ever found the other sixty-eight survivors, or the *Draeck* and her silver.

Now we were swimming among her bones. The first men to touch her remains in centuries. It was an awesome feeling.

'I wonder where the treasure lies?' I thought to myself, 'washed away over the reef maybe.'

When the foam cleared after the next wave I saw a new cave, higher and to the right. The walls were hung with red and yellow sponges and sprays of gorgonia coral.

I slid into it on the backwash, dragging my silver airline after me, and found the cave quite roomy inside. My exhaust bubbles were trapped under the roof, making bright silver puddles like mercury—the colour we had imagined the treasure would be. I looked quickly around for chests, or even piles of silver and gold doubloons. But there was nothing. Only a black rectangle of metal on the sandy floor.

Casually I picked it up, and was surprised by the weight. Reaching down I freed the diving knife in the sheath strapped on my leg and scratched experimentally at the edge of the metal. It glinted back at me, catching the light.

'Silver!' I breathed. And then, as a caution against disappointment I added, 'Or maybe lead.'

But I never really doubted, and as I rubbed away at the corrosion with a gloved thumb my heart thumped faster. Figures began to appear and a crown.

'PHILIPUS IIII' I read. 'REX HISPANIA' and the letters D.G. . . . Philip the Fourth, King of Spain, Deus Gratia, By the Grace of God! There was a date. 1652.

By now my hand was trembling for I knew what I had found. A figure 8 alongside a coat of arms confirmed it. Eight Reales . . . A Peso . . .

'A piece-of-eight!' I exclaimed and the bubbles puffed to the ceiling of the cave to make more silver puddles under the roof.

It was a Mexico piece-of-eight minted 311 years before, stamped from metal torn from the red earth of the South Americas by Indian slaves under the whips of Spanish overseers. It bore the Jerusalem Cross, the symbol of Spanish arms, and carried on the banners of Cortez and Pizarro. It was a symbol of the death of the Aztec and Inca civilizations. On the other side were the arms of the King of Spain at the time when he was the most powerful man in all the world— when he held dominion not only over his own Iberian provinces of Leon, Castille, Aragon and Granada, but also Portugal, Naples, Sicily, Belgium, and all of the Americas, North and South.

Powerful as he was, there were men who tweaked his beard and laughed at the yellow and red flag of Spain ('Old Pus and Blood', they called it) and shot holes in galleons. Men like Drake, Frobisher, Morgan, Anson, and the Dutchman Piet Heyn. They stole the king's pieces-of-eight or purchased them with

Pieces-of-eight; two cleaned and two straight from the ocean.

A candle and Bellarmine jug from the sand floor of the lower cave.

Draeck jugs and a candlestick on a winter shoreline.

Mexico piece-of-eight, 1654.

Cleaned coins glinting in the sun.

cannon shot, receipting them in blood. The silver caused a fever. A seaborne madness of lust and greed.

Though I had never seen one before, I knew them well enough from my childhood books. The rough silver coins that were the lifeblood of the Spanish Main. Long John Silver's parrot screeched at me down the years: 'Pieces-of-eight! Damn ye!' And down in that cold submarine cave below the Dragon Reef it seemed I could almost hear the measured tap of Silver's crutch.

'What wickedness have you seen, old coin?' I wondered as I tossed it in my hand, savouring the weight of it and feasting my eyes on its hard angular edges and the bright silver glint where I had tested it with the knife.

Looking down I saw the edge of another coin showing through the sand. I took off my glove and raked my fingers through the sand and found another— and yet another. The floor of the cave was studded with blackened silver. Pieces-of-four and two—smaller coins—as well as the larger eights.

I stuffed them down the sleeves of my rubber suit until they began falling out from sheer weight. Then I filled up one glove, then the other, and found still more silver.

When I was wondering where I could put it all there came a peremptory tug on the life-line. Then four tugs, clear and defined.

'Come back at once.' I knew the signal. Reluctantly I slid out of the cave and followed the life-line back to the boat. The sea had risen and the *Dorothy* was being thrown on her beam ends in the swell.

It was difficult getting aboard and I finally fell on to the deck with a whoop and an undignified and uncaring clatter of old silver coins. One of the divers had been thrown on the reef by a wave, but all of them had an expression on their faces I had never seen before, but would see again.

The grins were wide, ivory, from ear to ear, and there was a strange light in their eyes as they showed the coins they had found as well as the pottery, elephant tusks, and brass candlesticks.

As the *Dorothy* headed back towards the anchorage, buffeting her way through the wind-whipped waves with the spray flying across the decks, they passed a bottle of Queensland rum from the medical kit around. Gulping the fiery spirit, and shouting toasts above the noise of the diesel engine to pieces-of-eight and the Dragon treasure. It was a wonderful time.

Only Maurie Hammond did not smile.

'Dead men's silver' he said. 'There's no luck in it.'

A Shark Took My Leg

HENRI BOURCE

Henri Bource is a thirty-five-year-old underwater film maker and commercial diver specialising in submarine projects for oil companies.

He is also an accomplished musician, though he rarely plays now because of the pressure of diving work on off-shore oil and gas producing platforms.

A shark attack, an incident which would have terminated many people's diving careers forever, turned him from a week-end amateur diver into a full-time professional—an instance of courage and determination and a practical philosophy of life overcoming a handicap.

For Henri Bource, November 26th, 1964, began as a pleasant sort of day, the kind he most looked forward to. With forty other divers and friends from several clubs including his own Victorian Aqualung Club, he was one of a party aboard the fishing boat *Raemur-K*.

They were heading out from Port Fairy bound for Lady Julia Percy Island and the deck was crowded with divers and their gear.

It was a scene typical of many weekend dives as they approached the island. People struggling into wet-suits, adjusting harnesses, fiddling with gauges and loading cameras. All the last-minute things.

Henri, who was meticulous, had his gear ready early. In fact, most of it had been ready long before the trip. In the wheelhouse of the fishing boat he listened to the skipper Walter Kelly talking about the island with its colony of seals. The conversation inevitably turned to sharks. 'I've seen some big ones out here from this boat', said Kelly, telling them about some of his experiences. 'There's one in particular called Big Ben. He's been hanging around here for years.'

Henri Bource had never seen a shark up to that time, and had no reason to be afraid of them. He was fascinated by the fisherman's account and one of his ambitions was to get a really good shark sequence on cine film.

What a magnificent film shot one of the giant creatures Kelly had spoken of would make!

They reached the island, about eight kilometres off-shore and twenty-two kilometres or so from Port Fairy, an hour-and-a-half after leaving the wharf, and dropped anchor in the bay in the lee of Lady Julia Percy. The island was rocky with spectacular cliffs, and there were at least a thousand seals on the lower slopes. The acrid smell of ammoniac seal droppings drifted off-shore on the light breeze.

The fur seals set up a tremendous din, barking, squealing, and baying, as the boat approached. When Kelly anchored about 180 metres off-shore dozens of them flopped into the sea and came splashing out to meet them. It was everything an underwater photographer could wish for, and Henri Bource could hardly wait to get into the water.

His girl-friend Jill Ratcliffe was club safety officer for the day. She had the job of checking divers off as they went over the side. The first of them were soon sporting with the seals.

Jill Ratcliffe logged Henri's time of entry as 12.45 p.m. The club's safety regulations required him to swim with a partner if he wanted to use breathing apparatus. Since he was keen to get a camera record of the seals, and preferred to go on his own, he was free diving with a snorkel.

'I took a couple of quick breaths near a promising rock—I wanted the seals against a background—and dived', Henri remembers.

'Visibility was disappointing and I figured I would have to silhouette the seals against the surface to get effective results.

'So I positioned myself near the submerged rock, about ten metres down. Long fingers of kelp reached up for the surface. The visibility was even worse than I had thought. But the seals were helpful. I kept diving to a small ledge just below the rock and there I was able to film a number of seal cows, as they darted and spiralled through the long strands of kelp.

'All too soon I was out of film, so I swam back to the boat.'

He had hoped Jill would be able to have a dive. But at 1.30 p.m. she was still logging other divers and he decided to do some more free diving with the seals and join two other snorkel divers named Fred Arndt and Dietmar Kruppa. Together they found a large bull seal, floating on the surface, lying on his back with a hind flipper sticking out of the water and soaking in the sun. A seal at peace with the world.

'When we turned up he rolled a wary eye at the three of us, but was too lazy to move. Fred was the first to actually touch him. After a cautious ten minutes he accepted Dietmar and myself as well. It was one of those great and rare moments of communication with wild creatures. We thought it was pretty wonderful. Something to tell the others about when we got back.'

They began diving with him, and scratching him under the flippers. Suddenly and without warning the bull and all the nearby seals disappeared.

'The water was quite empty. I can remember it quite vividly', Henri says. 'There was a split second of eerie silence, and our instinct as divers warned us that something was wrong.'

They dived down about ten metres, hugging the bottom and looking around them. But they could not locate the seals.

'The premonition of imminent trouble was still very strong and as I came to the surface, I lifted my head out of the water, looking around to locate Fred and Dietmar. I was going to suggest that we'd better get back to the safety of the boat.

'Without any warning something hit me with tremendous force. I threw my arm up in the diver's signal for "Help!" and screamed "Shark . . . Shark!"

'Then I was torn through the water with enormous power and dragged below. The force of the attack ripped off my mask and snorkel. I could only make out a blurred shape, a huge shadow, as the shark took me down to the bottom, and I felt that it gripped me by the leg.

'As it dived deep, the shark shook me, the way a dog would shake an old slipper. The pain was unbearable. I found myself reaching for the shark's eyes in a desperate attempt to escape. But I could barely reach my arm around his gigantic snout, and I just scrabbled helplessly across the monster's muzzle.

'There was another sensation in which the pain and fear were almost forgotten. I was drowning. I needed air. Suffocating as I was tugged and rolled from side to side.

'Then suddenly it all stopped. The shaking and the turmoil ceased.

'There was a moment almost of peace. Then I realised, as I groped for the surface, that I had just had my leg bitten off.

'The air was wonderful as I gasped on the surface. Then I felt down to the remains of my left leg. I was quite calm. Shock perhaps. But I found it hard to focus clearly. There was a curious division in which my body tended towards natural animal panic. But my mind remained quite detached and calm.'

Dietmar Kruppa was the first to Henri's side. The injured diver clutched at his shoulder, trying to catch his breath again. He tried to speak but no words came. The blood tasted sweet in his mouth, as it clouded the water. Then he realised the shark would attack again and, afraid they would not be able to see it coming in the blood, he tried to push himself away from Dietmar so that he would not be hit too.

The shark came back at least five times. But Fred Arndt and Dietmar, who, showing tremendous courage, fought the monster off with their light metal hand spears, meant for little fish, not killer sharks a tonne in weight. They were bent and twisted out of shape afterwards. But despite their repeated jabs the shark did not attack either Arndt or Kruppa.

As often happens in an attack the shark kept trying to get to its original victim, held up and now barely conscious between the two other divers.

But now the *Raemur-K* was bearing down on them.

As soon as the cry 'Shark!' was heard and the welling cloud of blood was seen on board, Walter Kelly hit the starter button of the motor and surged the boat towards them without even waiting to pick up the anchor. He dragged it with the boat's power, and as they drew close, without hesitation Jill Ratcliffe grabbed the safety line, jumped in and swam towards the struggling group in the blood-stained water. Others jumped in alongside her with no thought of their own safety.

At the side of the boat, Jill called for a rope. Quickly, two of the divers entered the water and fastened the line around Henri. But they couldn't lift his weight out of the water. 'In a last desperate attempt, I slid my arm up the rope, and I felt a hard grip on my wrist. Colin Watson, a policeman, grabbed my arm and jerked me on board, spraying blood across the deck.'

The sight was almost too much for some of the others, who were unaware that Henri Bource had lost his leg. It was hardly pleasant for those in the water. Apart from what must have been a ghastly sight, they realised that they were now left in the water in a pool of blood with the shark still around.

Colin Watson and others carried Henri to the middle of the deck and immediately began to apply a tourniquet and first aid. 'I remember only the dark shapes of wet suits and the occasional face above me, registering horror. Not until the moment I'd been taken on board did anyone realise the terrible extent of my injury. The shark had severed my leg at the knee.

'Faces closed in around me as I was laid full-length on the timber decking. Frequent spasms of pain shot through my legs. Someone held my head for comfort and they found a pillow from somewhere. My most vivid recollections now are of the faces; they all looked at me with disbelief. Their shocked expressions seemed to say, "This couldn't be happening. This is the sort of thing you only read about!".'

Divers applying torniquet to Henri on fishing boat deck.

Genuine shots from film taken at the time.

Despite the horror of the situation the helpers' first aid was coolly and efficiently applied, and the swift placing of the tourniquet was to prove vital in the drama which followed. There was an agony of indecision while they decided whether to pick up people still on the island or run for port. Then on the way back to Port Fairy, Walter Kelly dodged through reefs and lines of craypots on the shortest possible route home. As it turned out every minute counted in what was literally a race for Henri Bource's life. After the cruel ill-chance of the encounter with the shark he had some lucky breaks.

By the time they got under way the initial shock had diminished a little and Henri Bource could distinguish voices. Somebody was at the radio, calling for an ambulance and a doctor to be standing by at the Port Fairy landing. He heard them tell the shore-based operator that his blood group was unknown, and lifting his head a little he managed to whisper the blood group to somebody above him and a moment later heard it was radioed ashore. This was one of the things which made the hairline of difference between life and death.

'Actually my mind was not unclear and I was conscious of the people standing around. But my vision was fading and I could see the people only as vague shapes. Someone still had hold of me, keeping me as motionless as possible as the boat dipped and rolled in the choppy sea, and it came to me that even though I was safe on board, the trip back to Port Fairy would take about one and a half hours. A long time without medical aid. That was the last clear thought I had for some time.'

The sick excitement of shock was ebbing away from the pit of his stomach. In its place another feeling was developing. Peace. He recognised this for what it was.

'By this time we had reached the half-way mark; I knew I was dying. I felt a great temptation to relax—to meet the calmness that was creeping over me. At first it was pleasant. Then instinct told me that it was approaching death and I began to fight. I heard whispers around me and asked how much longer it would take to reach shore. At first the words choked in my throat and someone lowered their face to me. After several attempts I managed the question. The face replied, "Not long now . . . you'll be alright, Henri." I don't think whoever said it really believed it.

'The remainder of the journey was a continual struggle to fight the haze closing in on me. I managed to keep semi-conscious throughout the rest of the trip. I remember a voice in the unreality surrounding me commenting, "Isn't it incredible . . . He's still conscious".

'The next sensation was of a light thud, then the rubber suit was being torn from my arm and someone was applying a blood pressure apparatus. I felt a needle plunge into my flesh, and looked up to see a man's worried face.'

Then another injection was given to him and he was ready to receive the transfusion—the life-giving liquid.

Henri did not know at this stage that he had lost three and a half litres of blood. Taken from the normal four and a half litres held in the human system it didn't leave much to go on with. Doctors said later that if the journey had taken only a little longer, or he had lost a fraction more blood, he would have passed the point of no-return.

The ambulance rushed him to the new Warrnambool Hospital.

'I remember the long passage, the hum of the elevator, the nurses and the rubber suit being cut from me—that hurt a bit, for it had cost hard-earned savings. After two hours I was ready for the operating theatre.

'I awoke with my mind still foggy from the anaesthetic. Only nineteen hours had elapsed since the four-metre white shark had torn my leg from my body and my eyes focused slowly on the cage holding the bedclothes away from my legs. Then I looked at the space where only yesterday my leg had been.'

'My leg had gone and there wasn't a damned thing I could do about it.'

In the ten years since he has had plenty of time to think about it all.

'There are no vain regrets', Henri says. 'I don't believe in wasting time on worrying over things which can't be changed and I have adapted myself well enough. I don't think I've got any hang-ups.

'I still dive, of course. In fact I was diving again three weeks later, if you can believe it. They got me out on a series of publicity stunts to try to catch the shark.

'They took big lines and gallons of bullock's blood. But the whole thing soured me off badly because fishermen shot some seals to try to bring the shark around. They didn't get the shark and it was sad about the seals.

Henri in 1974 working on Bass Strait oil rig.

'Personally I have nothing against that shark or any shark in general. They do what Nature intended them to do and they don't kill as indiscriminately as man or for the sheer pleasure of it.

'I've seen quite a few white sharks since that day, making films, and far from being a marine horror they are really very beautiful. I admire them.

'The attack changed my life of course. There's no getting away from it. But in some ways it was for the better. Before I was a bit irresponsible. I liked the good life, wine, girls, and didn't think too hard about tomorrow. It brought the realities home to me sharply.

'I made a film about the incident called *Savage Shadows*. It wasn't too painful to make because I was immersed in the technical camera side and it actually worried some of the other divers far more in the re-enactment scenes (especially getting back in the water at that place) than me.

'I've made other films since, and things have gone well. I don't suppose I'll ever forget November 26th, 1964, as long as I live. But—well, that's Life I guess, and if there's one thing I learned out of it all it's that it's great to be alive.'

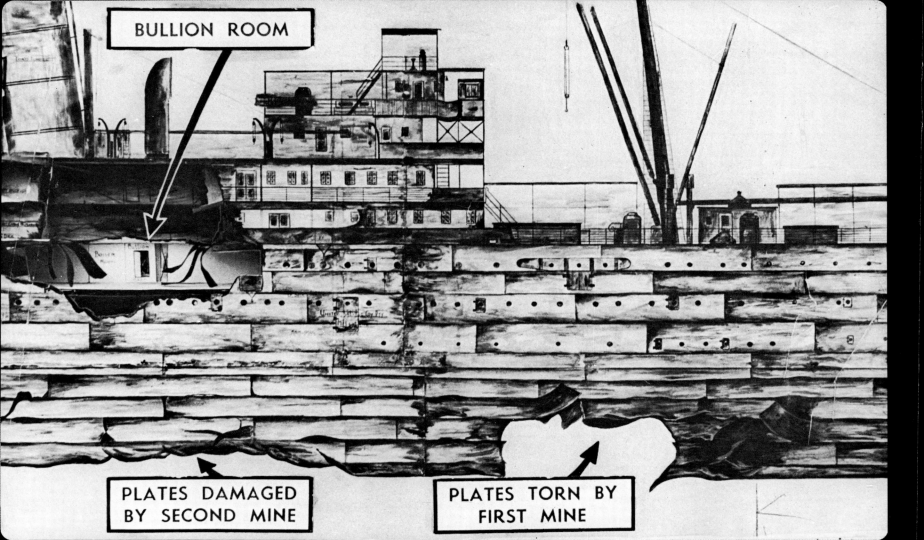

BULLION ROOM

PLATES DAMAGED BY SECOND MINE

PLATES TORN BY FIRST MINE

The Niagra Gold

JOHNNO JOHNSTONE

When the stately old trans-Pacific liner R.M.S. *Niagra* struck a German mine forty-eight kilometres off Whangarei Harbour, New Zealand, on June 19th, 1940, she settled in 134 metres of water.

The 14,000-ton veteran of twenty-seven years plying between Sydney and San Francisco sank gently. She took no lives when she made her final plunge. But deep in her strong room were eight and a half tons of gold ingots worth £2,500,000 sterling in 1940 and nearly $9,000,000 today.

In 1940, the bars stamped with the mark of South Africa's Rand mines were more important even than their monetary value. They were being used to buy American aircraft, tanks, guns and munitions for a desperate Britain and in a troubled world, gold was the only currency the U.S. would accept. Within a few hours of the news of the *Niagra*'s sinking Whitehall in London was calling for reports on the feasibility of a salvage operation.

The reports were pessimistic. It was generally considered that the gold would be unsalvagable. Where in Australia, in wartime, could a ship and gear and men with the skill to attempt the world's deepest salvage be found . . . ?

As it turned out their address was in Melbourne. The firm was the United Salvage Company with Captain John Williams as surface controller of operations, and John 'Johnno' Johnstone as chief diver. The legend on Johnstone's business cards read DIVING—ANYWHERE, ANY DEPTH.

When the *Niagra* salvage was put to the company as a proposition, Johnstone pointed out that it was deeper than anyone had ever worked before. Then he said, 'OK. We'll do it.'

The morning of October 18 was a total failure. Visibility was zero. The bell went down into water dark as a tomb, so that Johnstone peering out into the murk through the armour-glass parts did not see the wreck until he felt the jolt of her plates under his feet.

'Take her up again', he said, and they could hear the disappointment in his voice.

They winched him 122 metres back to the surface and the sunlight again and unbolted the bronze dome from above his head in a mood of general pessimism. Few words were spoken and the diver stumped away to his quarters.

About noon Johnstone said he wanted to try again. The change of tide might have cleared the water. The steam winches groaned on the *Claymore*'s deck,

31

The bell surfaces from the wreck.

the white cylinder with its dumbell top swung out over the sea, and disappeared again on the end of its wire deep, deep down to where the *Niagra* lay on the sea-bed far below.

This time Johnstone's voice came through on the telephone to Captain Williams up on the bridge with a more cheerful note.

'This is better, skipper', he said. 'I think we may be able to give it a go.'

There was a silence while they waited impatiently on deck to hear more. Then Johnstone's voice came through again. 'I can see the strong room, skipper', he said. 'The explosives have opened it up nicely.' The sound of the bell settling once more on the sloping side of the sunken ship came clearly up the wires.

'Send down the small grab', ordered the diver, in the way a surgeon would ask for forceps. The grab was a metre wide, the jaws painted white, and it was almost as wide as the strong room door.

'Hold it!' said Johnstone. They could hear him as clearly as though he were in the room next door. 'More to the right . . . Over a bit more. That's it. Now drop her'.

There was a loud ringing of metal as the grap dangling on its wire struck the door edge. Then it disappeared inside the black hole of the entrance.

'Take a bite!' commanded Johnstone, voice tense.

Twice he said, 'No good', as he heard the grab gnash its metal teeth against steel. On the third time he heard the sound of splintering wood.

'Take her up slow!' he commanded. 'Very slow—I want a good look.'

Up came the grab, through the door at the bottom of the gaping twenty-metre hole the explosives had made in the ship. Johnstone strained his eyes in the twilight 122 metres down, trying to see in the shadows what it was the grab gripped in its jaws.

There was a long silence. 'Take up the bell', he said finally.

'Johnno, what the hell is it?' Williams' voice came impatiently down through the earphones. 'Wake up man. Can't you hear me?'

'I can hear you all right, skipper.' The voice was cautious. 'I just thought I saw a box in the grab.'

The gold was stored in boxes. Two bars to a box . . .

Up went the bell. The spanners rattled and clanged eagerly on its lid as the deck crew got Johnno out of his steel cell in record time, and then everyone fell silent except Captain Jim Herd giving orders on the grab winch. The wire

"SALVAGE FROM £684,000/- WORTH

£684,000 worth of gold from the wreck R.M.S. *Niagra*.

SEA"

GOLD BULLION FROM

wound in gently and softly with the grab and they waited breathless to see what it held.

The deck crew reached out as it broke the surface to prevent the grab jarring or striking the rail. Dead centre over the deck the grab hiccoughed, unlocked its iron jaws, and spewed out a mouthful of foul-smelling mud. And a box.

It had hardly hit the deck before eager hands tore it open. There, gleaming in the sun magnificent and untarnished, lay two bars of gold with the Rand gold mines stamp on their gleaming surfaces!

Cheer after cheer rang out across the water. Men danced, and jumped and hugged each other, for this was the dazzling moment of success. The visible proof that the job everyone had said was impossible could be accomplished.

The many weeks and months of back-breaking preparation now seemed worthwhile and the black mood of the morning had vanished. Though these were only the first two bars, they knew now that they would get the others. Or at least enough to make it all worthwhile.

Down in the rat-hole saloon of the old *Claymore* they celebrated the *Niagra* gold. John Williams, his assistant Captain Jim Herd, Johnno Johnstone and his brother and diving partner Bill, borrowed from the Navy for the job, and the deck crew. Photographs thirty-three years old still show the gleam of those first two bars of gold on the saloon table and the triumphant grins of the *Claymore* crew.

By the end of the month they had fifteen boxes. In November they got forty-six boxes in one day, and 246½ boxes for the month. By December 8, with

Each box contained sixty-eight pounds of gold, valued at £8,460, and the total 1941 value of the salvage was £2,397,600. The job was accomplished in twelve months, from December 9, 1940, to December 8, 1941. The delicate job of blasting a hole in the vessel to expose the strongroom 7·6 m deep in the ship took eight months, the actual salvage of the gold less than two.

It was not only the deepest effective salvage in the history of the world. It was also one of the most efficient.

And it was conducted during wartime in the middle of a German minefield.

'Those mines gave us some bad moments', says John Johnstone today. At eighty-one his mind and memory are still clear, his handshake firm. He made his last dive at the age of seventy-two, and age has treated him kindly.

'Yes, those mines', he said. 'They were the worst part of the whole show.

Loading the bell with soda-lime canisters used to purify the air of carbon dioxide.

33

When we went looking for the *Niagra* it was generally believed she had been sabotaged. Sunk by a bomb in her cargo. No one thought of mines.

'In the early part of the search the old *Claymore* was steaming on the surface and I was swinging along, 300 feet down in the bell, looking out of the windows for wreckage. I saw a number of dark disc-like shapes, but since my mind was set on the *Niagra* they didn't really register with me.

'It was only when my bell was fouled by a wire that I realised their significance. At first I heard it scraping on the outside of the bell and thought it must be a loose wire from the ship, used in dragging for the wreck. I said so on the 'phone, and the deck crew checked all around the *Claymore* but couldn't find anything dangling over.

' "Nothing loose up here, Johnno", said the skipper. I could tell he was hoping it was a wire from the *Niagra*. But suddenly the wire came across my window and with an awful chill I realised what it was. It was a square wire, with serrations on the corners. I had seen such wire before in England in the first World War. Tether lines of German manufacture, with the serrations for cutting the paravane wires of mine sweepers.

' "My God!" I said to myself, "It's a mine!"

'It dawned on me at once that the discs we had seen were mine anchors, and in our search we had been steaming unwittingly through the middle of a minefield. So that was what had sunk the *Niagra*!

'But while that particular mystery was solved I was more anxious at that moment for our own safety. With that mine anchor line fouled around my bell there was a live explosive-filled mine somewhere between me and the *Claymore*.

'If it was powerful enough to sink the 14,000-ton *Niagra* there wasn't much hope for me or the *Claymore* if it should go off.

'Trying to keep cool and think about it I reasoned that there were a number of alternatives, most of them unpleasant. The mine could simply blow me and the bell to pieces. The wire could cut my wire with its serrated edges. Or the mine could blow our whole outfit, the *Claymore*, surface crew, and yours truly Johnno Johnstone in his bell, to little pieces, scattering us all over Harauki Gulf.

' "Keep calm, lad" I said to myself. "You've been in bad spots before. Maybe there's a way out of this one too."

'There was. From the way the wire was angled it looked as though it might be fouled around the bell in a loop. If we lifted gently the bell just might slide out of it.

' "Heave very slowly", I ordered.

' "What's wrong, Johnno? What is it?" Captain Williams kept asking on the phone. He could tell from my voice that something was very wrong.

' "I'm fouled by a wire", I said, briefly, giving no more information than before. Why worry the deck crew unnecessarily. If we were unlucky they would find out soon enough. The bell began to go up gently, an inch or two at a time. I had my hands over my ears waiting for the explosion—though I never would have heard it. Then, suddenly outside my window I saw the mine itself swaying and bobbing, black and ugly, with its deadly horns just waiting for a contact.

' "What's wrong down there?" Captain Williams asked again. But my words stuck in my throat. I could only watch in a horrified sort of way as the mine swung clear like a big lazy animal and drifted down-current.

' "Pull me up", I managed at last in a hoarse croak. "All clear."

'Realising the problem the mine might create with the crew's morale I said nothing when they got me out of the bell, though my face spoke volumes.

'"Well, Johnno", said Captain Williams quietly later on when we were alone in the saloon. "What's the mystery of the wire?"

' "No mystery", I replied. "We're in the middle of a bloody minefield."

'We remained at anchor, wondering what to do about it. While we lay-to one of the crew saw something over the side. "There's a sunfish!" he said. "You don't often see them!"

'It was no sunfish, but another mine. While we were heaving in our anchor, next day, I was at the anchor head when I saw something that made me yell to the winch crew, "Stop! Stop heaving!"

'The mine cable was round our anchor chain, the mine itself, rusty and green with weed, bobbing close to the ship. We slacked off, and the mine disappeared again.

' "We mustn't panic on this, Johnno", the skipper said. "The crew will have to be told."

'They took it very well. We decided to call over one of the Royal New Zealand Navy minesweepers in the area. Because it was wartime and replacements were impossible to get we couldn't afford to lose the anchor and chain which were vital to the operation. It was agreed that the crew would be evacuated

The *Claymore* above the wreck with all her improvised derricks, winches, and lifting gear.

and I should go down in standard diving dress and attempt to unshackle the mine and attach another line which would be used to tow the mine away to where it could be destroyed by the minesweeper.

'All very well in theory, but the practice turned out to be somewhat more difficult. There was a confusion in the signals on the tow-line and the line tightened bringing the mine hard up alongside me, and jamming me against the ship—the sandwich between the horned ball of deadly explosives and the steel bow of the vessel.

'In near panic, I grabbed two of the horns in my hands and—with the swell buffeting me cruelly against the ship's side—endeavoured to keep the horns from coming in contact with either the ship or my own copper helmet.

'The situation lasted less than a minute, but to me it seemed to be forever before the mine surged back to the depths and I was hauled aboard again. My physical bruises were nothing to the dents in my courage and confidence.

' "We won't ask you to do that again, Johnno", said Captain Williams, and I don't know that I really could have gone down again that day.

'In the end they freed the mine by backing *Claymore* off with a slack anchor line and having the HMNZS *Humphrey* pass close by with her sweeping gear.

With luck a paravane cut the mine wire and it was sunk by rifle fire, sending a huge yellow column of water, smoke and spray fifty feet in the air.

'It took me a day or two to get over the episodes of the mines. I was glad when the weather broke and we had to go into Whangarei for a few days.'

The most remarkable aspect of the *Niagra* salvage was the way wartime difficulties were overcome. There were no suitable ships at all available, because every seaworthy craft was already pressed into naval service.

Captain Williams found the *Claymore* at Auckland, an old coastal steamer built in Scotland in 1902 and derelict for three years. Her decks had grass growing on them. Her entire upper structure was white with bird lime, and the bridge covered in bird nests. All her gear had been stripped or stolen, including her helm and steering gear, and even the engine room telegraph.

Since all maritime equipment had been requisitioned for Navy use, they had to find replacements from junk yards. In the end the *Claymore* was a masterpiece of improvisation, and allowing for the limitation of her size, did an excellent job.

In fact a bigger vessel might have been fatal. The German mines round the wreck were set at five metres below the surface. The *Niagra* drew eight and a half metres but the little *Claymore* drawing only 2·7 metres skipped unsuspectingly over the top of the minefield even as it claimed another victim—one of the Navy minesweepers, the *Puriri*, with the loss of five lives and eleven badly injured.

The diving was shared between Johnno Johnstone and his brother Bill, a member of HMAS *Sydney*'s crew, and released for the salvage. Between them they were to make 316 descents to the wreck. The operation, risky as it may have seemed, probably saved Bill's life. The *Sydney* was sunk with all hands in November 1941 in the Indian Ocean by the German raider *Kormeran* while Bill was working on the *Niagra* gold.

The bell, which was the main instrument of success, was remarkable in its own way. Designed in Melbourne by David Isaacs, it was 2·7 metres high, one and a half metres wide at the bottom, and came up to a mushroom top with fourteen quartz glass windows and a top-entry hatch.

No air was fed from the surface. It was designed to work at surface pressure to get away from decompression problems and risk of the bends. In effect it was like a captive submarine. The divers breathed the air sealed inside it, using soda-lime canisters and oxygen to purify the air of carbon dioxide.

They could work comfortably for four hours at a time at depths over 120 m, which would have been impossible for a helmet diver or one working on SCUBA because of pressure changes.

The disadvantage of the bell was that the diver could only be an observer and could not take an active part in operations. But this was overcome by skilfully directing grabs and bundles of explosives from the ship above.

The bell—which still exists in the United Salvage Company's store sheds in Melbourne in 1974—weighed nearly three tonnes together with its heavy metal ballast. If the wire broke the divers could release the 272 kg of iron ballast from fastenings inside the bell and float to the surface.

'Or so we hoped!' Johnstone wryly noted in his journal.

Early in the search for the *Niagra* he made one descent to 160·9 m which was in 1940—and probably still is thirty-four years later—a southern hemisphere depth record.

'It was far more comfortable than a standard diving suit', Johnstone says. 'We tested it first with sandbags and it never leaked a drop. It was designed to go to 750 feet and I was always completely confident in the bell and the surface crew. I wouldn't have dived if I hadn't been.'

The divers were always in touch by a phone system working off vibrator pads on their larynx to leave their mouths clear for using the respirator. The phone apparatus was designed by the PMG Research Section in Melbourne, and worked brilliantly—which was just as well, for without it nothing could have been accomplished at all.

There were a number of early problems with the bell. One was a spinning motion which made the unhappy occupants violently seasick. This was solved by plaiting wires to prevent the turning. Another was the jerking up and down as *Claymore* rode to swells up to six metres high. This was never entirely eliminated, but was partly solved by a shock absorber system on one of the masts.

Having got the *Claymore* into a sea-going condition and perfected their diving gear, the next job was to find the *Niagra*. This was no easy task for she lay inside an area defined only as twenty-three kilometres square.

For weeks they steamed up and down trailing trawl gear in the hope of snagging the wreck. It was during this period that the misadventures with the mines occurred. Eventually they were successful—when crewman Billy Green steered a wrong course, due south.

'Hell's bells!' cried Captain Williams looking at the compass. 'You're way off course, man. Bring her round!'

He had hardly spoken the words when there was a crash of wire and steel outriggers collapsing at the stern. The *Claymore* was hooked hard and solid by her wires to something on the bottom. It was the *Niagra*. The date was January 31st, 1941, two months after the start of operations. The next dive, with Johnno Johnstone going down to identify the obstruction, was nearly the end of the whole thing.

Johnstone had gone down below the 100 m mark. There was a shout over the telephone, 'Hold the bell!' The wire jerked taut to a stop. 'What is it?' asked Williams anxiously. 'It's her—the *Niagra*!' came Johnstone's voice. 'I can see two funnels and a mast . . .'

She was lying over on her port side, the sea bed strewn with debris. Tins, suitcases, luggage, splintered wood. There were two huge holes in her side. One from the first mine which had sunk her, and another from one she must have struck on her way down, else there would have been few survivors.

Johnno in the bell sketched busily on a pad everything he saw, for the information would be vital in the salvage plan, and it was important to precisely locate the area of the strong room where the gold was stored.

At that moment one of the most dangerous episodes of the whole salvage occurred. The *Claymore*'s bow mooring parted, and the ship swung violently off downwind, dragging Johnson in the bell bouncing and clanging along the side of the wreck.

The wire missed a set of hooked davits by millimetres; the bell bounced clear across the ragged edges of the huge hole made by the mine. The bell finished upside down in the mud and slime of the sea bed, before the wire slack could be taken in and Johnstone hauled to safety.

If the bell had dropped into the hole caused by the mine with its inward-curving edges of sharp steel, the wire would probably have sheared and the bell been caught in the depths of the wreck forever, together with its occupant.

Johnstone was bleeding from the battering when they opened his hatch on deck. 'Don't ever', he said, 'Don't EVER do that again!' Then he managed a grin and they knew he was alright.

Once the wreck was found, the next job was to gain entry to the strong room put into the ship. This took eight months of blasting, removing debris with the grabs, and blasting again. The charges had to be strong enough to cut through the heavy plate, but not so strong that they would rupture the far side of the strongroom divided from the engine room only by a partition.

If the partition had collapsed the gold would have fallen deep into the engines, scattered among pistons, sumps, and catwalks, and would probably have become impossible to reach.

But by working carefully and patiently over the intervening months the hole in the ship was gradually enlarged until it was twenty metres long, nine metres wide, and eight metres deep in the ship. Only then was the strong room door exposed.

In the process the team had become experts at their jobs. A movement of a few millimetres with the bell or grabs was critical and the *Claymore* had to be positioned precisely over the wreck, and kept in station despite wind and the rise and fall of the Pacific swell.

They kept her in place by eight concrete moorings, alternately tightening and slackening wires to her ordinary cargo winches to the instructions of the divers Johnno and Bill Johnstone taking their shifts below.

Once the ship was right, the grabs and the explosives had to be lowered. To rid themselves of the uncomfortable motion the divers actually sat the bell on the sloping side of the wreck with a slack wire. Captain Williams grumbled about the risk, but it undoubtedly made for more accurate observations. But there was one bad day when Bill Johnstone's wires fouled and for more than one hour he was hooked to the wreck while those above tried every move to free the wire. Luck was with him and by coolness he was freed.

They made a cardboard scale model of the ship and tore away pieces to mark their progress. The moorings continually shifted, they were racked by the winter storms, and once came within a few metres of being wrecked on one of the Gulf Islands.

But by October 10th, 1941, they were at the bullion room door. By the 12th they had blown it off, and now the real reward for their labours began. They used a special grab for the gold, designed and built in Whangarei by Williams and Johnstone.

There was always the worry that they were in the wrong part of the ship, despite the detailed plans they had been given.

When the grab came up with a teapot, an ice-bucket, a salt cruet and knives and forks, Williams was beside himself.

'You're in the saloon!' he accused the divers. But on the same day a door came up in the grab. It was unquestionably the strong room door.

Next day they got to the gold and by the time of the last dive on December 8, 1941, they accomplished a ninety-four per cent salvage where a zero result had been forecast.

'It wasn't the gold itself', Johnstone says, looking back down the long years of a lifetime of diving with faraway eyes. 'True it glittered prettily on the deck, untarnished by the sea, and you could feel the power and the fascination it might have for men. But really it was just a symbol. Metal with no practical purpose dug up out of one hole in the ground to go back into another—the vaults.

'But though you might say we risked our lives for it there was more than just the gold to it all. There was the companionship of the best team of men you could ever work with.' He pauses. 'And there was the other thing. The satisfaction of doing a job so deep they said it couldn't be done.'

Salvage ship *Claymore* at Whanarei with gold aboard.

An Eel Named Harry

VALERIE TAYLOR

The blonde, blue-eyed other half of the successful Taylor underwater film partnership, combines apparent feminine fragility with a tough commonsense approach to diving.

She has been a commercial artist, an actress playing the lead role in the play *Seven Year Itch* during its nine-month run in Sydney, the Australian women's spearfishing champion for three successive years in the 1960s, and is now a marine photographer with displays in most major magazines including the U.S. *National Geographic*.

Valerie has appeared in many Australian and overseas television productions and played a main part (she was the only woman) in the recent American feature film *Blue Water, White Death*. This motion picture, made by Peter Gimbel in 1970 on the search for the great white shark, is probably the most successful and technically accurate diving film ever made.

Valerie's restless energy and artist's eye for a balanced picture are her greatest assets, along with an intuitive feeling for the marine creatures which are her subjects.

'Moray eels are nice people', says Valerie Taylor. You look into those deep saucer blue eyes to make sure she's not kidding. She isn't.

'They're quite gentle', she goes on, 'if you handle them properly. Mind you, Harry (one of the eels at Heron Island) bit a visiting cameraman on the knee last year.'

She giggles. 'But knowing the fellow in question I'd say he showed good taste.'

Valerie has an affection for all fish. The weird and wonderful, savage and apparently nasty included. She greatly admires sharks, for their power and streamlined beauty and considers them to be among the most misunderstood of living creatures.

Sharks, because of their roaming pelagic nature, and instinctive, unreasoning behaviour, are almost untamable. But morays are different, quite easy to domesticate, despite their evil reputation which Valerie says is largely undeserved.

History has been against them, for one thing. Legends linger on of the Roman Caesars throwing screaming slaves and Christians to a ghastly death in squirming pools of famished morays. In modern times their simulated rage when disturbed has earned them a bad reputation. They tend to come popping open-mouthed

Val Taylor.

Mildred the manta obligingly towing a diver.

out of holes in the coral like bared-teeth jack-in-the-boxes. The aim—usually successful—is to frighten away intruders on their territory. It's unnerving until you get used to it.

Also they look a bit like snakes and this is no doubt behind the mistaken belief that their bite is poisonous.

'But really they're much maligned', Valerie protests. 'They're shy and very easily frightened. The show of ferocity they put on is large a defensive bluff, like most wild creatures.

Valerie gives names to all her pet fish at Heron Island on the Great Barrier Reef. This is where the Taylors do much of their filming for their television programme *Taylors Innerspace*. 'We spent nine months at Heron once and eventually got to know almost everybody down there.' (When she says that you know she means fish.) 'Harry and Fang, the two moray eels, the angel fish Big Fred, and Little Fred, and Mildred the manta ray.

Though often reported as 4.3 to six metres across, Mildred in fact is about 2.4 to 2.7 metres from wing tip to wing tip. This is still a big manta, and she is quite heavy at 226 kilos or more. Which causes another problem.

'She loves to be scratched on the tummy. Her skin is rough and wears out my finger nails. I don't mind that. But it sends her into mad ecstacies. She gets a silly soulful look on her face and stops swimming, and floats to the bottom on top of me looking ga-ga, while I wriggle frantically trying to get out from underneath.'

'Mildred is quite happy to have divers handle her and even to tow them around. Once the divers even parked a two-man submarine on her back.'

The Taylors have found that the reef fish, particularly cod, are intelligent and easily trained.

'Once a cod learns a trick he doesn't forget easily. There was a particular red cod who I thought would make a marvellous picture against the background of a yellow cup coral. I began feeding him and then worked him over to the coral area. Then I refused to feed him anywhere else.

'It wasn't long before he got the idea, and stationed himself beautifully. I got the series of pictures I wanted. But it proved a little more expensive that I'd bargained for.

'Every time he saw me after that he'd dash over and pose beautifully along-side the coral. He was so splendid I always felt I had to reward him—and such

a good picture that I kept taking shot after shot and using up far more film than I ever needed. If I dived in at that place on the reef tomorrow I bet he'd still be there, and that he'd whisk over with a flick of the tail to pose alongside the yellow coral.'

Valerie tells some moving stories of relationships between fish themselves. They're far from being 'cold fish' as is popularly imagined.

At one time on the Barrier Reef she and Ron were working from a barge. A school of thirteen kingfish stationed themselves under it, and made it their home for a time. One day Valerie noticed that one of the kingfish had been hurt by a shark or other big fish. It was badly slashed. Half its stomach had been torn away, and Ron did not expect it to live.

Next day most of the school of kingfish were gone, out on the deep reefs fishing. The sick one stayed behind under the protective shadow of the barge, and one healthy kingfish remained too. When they dived to look at the sick fish the healthy one shepherded it away, and got between it and the divers.

When the barge was moved for filming the invalid and his escort turned up soon after. Every day the pattern was the same. The school went out and returned later in the day. Valerie was sure that different kingfish took turns to stay with the sick fish.

'For a long time he was very feeble', she says. 'But gradually he picked up strength, the wounds healed and he began to move more briskly. Finally there came the day when all the kingfish went fishing.'

The eels were her favourites at Heron. Harry was the first to become tame. While she was feeding fish he would put his head out of a hole in the coral, and little by little Valerie won his confidence.

'At first he was very nervous and used to pretend he was a very ferocious dragon—opening his mouth wide and waving his head around. But I persuaded him to stop that nonsense, and after a while he became so docile I could reach into his hole and pull him out, and have him twine around my arms and neck and peer into my mask.'

Morays normally hate to leave their holes, and it was a mark of great confidence that Harry allowed himself to be drawn completely out.

'He was very gentle taking food. He'd just take it delicately from your fingers, never snatching like Fang. And Harry was a great smoocher. He loved to nuzzle up to me. Fang became tame after watching Harry. But she has never been quite as confident about being handled.

'Harry's quite funny at feeding time. Sometimes I pretend I can't see him and he keeps popping up in front of my mask from holes in the coral with a "Here I am!" expression on his face. You push him back in one hole and he pops out of another, waving for attention.

'Morays change colour, and poor Harry goes through all shades of speckled anxiety if I ignore him. Fang is much less demonstrative. Like people, they have their own personalities.

'They're both quite big as morays go, I guess. About five feet long and maybe six inches thick. They look different from each other, of course. But even if you didn't know them well you could pick them apart because Fang has had a damaged lip and a protruding tooth.

'Ugly? How could anyone think they're ugly! They're beautiful, charming and delightful creatures.' She laughs. 'But I guess beauty is really only skin deep and it's their personalities which appeal to me.'

A part of her past she seldom mentions now is that she and her husband were both Australian Spearfishing Champions—Ron won the world title at Tahiti in 1965.

'It would be silly to waste time in vain regrets' she explains. 'Ron won four successive Australian championships at a time when Australian spearfishing was at its best. As well as the world title. And we were very proud of him.

'But it saddened us when we saw the effect spearfishing was having. No one ever dreamed when spearfishing began how quickly it could denude whole areas and upset the ecology. Now we're conservationists and hardly ever pull a trigger. We're much prouder of our photography. The modern trend is all against undersea hunting and personally I'm glad.

'Remember too that Hans Haas and Jaques Cousteau and the others also began as hunters. But no one who's at all sensitive can spend a long time in the sea and not come to love the creatures in it.'

She laughs, remembering the time she kept a pet four and a half kilo crayfish in her parents' salt water swimming pool, and an octopus she fed crabs which used to follow her along the shore. 'Perhaps I'm an extremist. An eccentric. Like people who talk to the trees.'

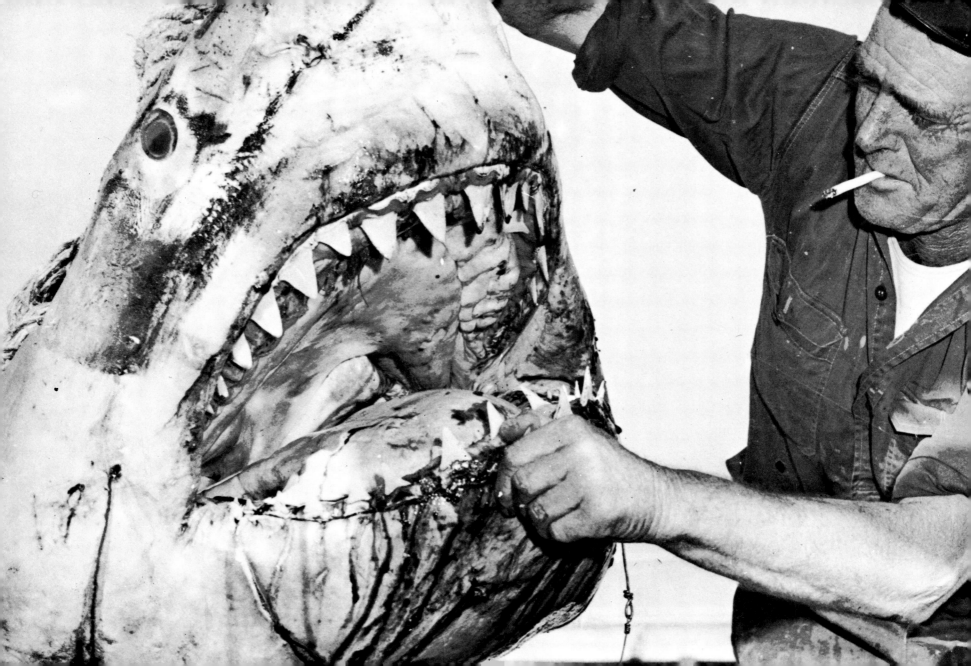

The Shark Fisherman

HUGH EDWARDS

Ted Nelson was a shark fisherman who worked out of Fremantle and off the shores of Rottnest Island.

He was skilled in all the facets of his trade. Deft with a hook and line, swift in tying a knot, adept at coaxing a sullen diesel, predicting the weather or handling a tiller.

But beyond these things he also had a deep knowledge of marine creatures and an accumulation of sea lore which he was generous in imparting. At Fremantle, a port of many shark fishermen, they called him Sharkey Nelson. A tribute in itself.

Sharkey Nelson's mast-head light used to go dipping through the harbour blackness between three and four o'clock in the morning. The boat, which was called *Shaleen*, was invisible in the darkness except for her white top light, the red and green port and starboard lanterns and the faint glow of Sharkey's cigarette where he stood at the wheel.

By the time she reached the harbour mouth, with its twin lighthouses and flashing beacons, the first pale streaks of dawn would be showing astern in the east. *Shaleen* would begin to lift her bows rhythmically to the new day and the swells of the open sea.

At full daylight she would be lying-to, drifting for bait fish on the offshore reefs. Sharkey would be at his accustomed place amidships, one pace back from the gunwhale so that the fish could not see him, and working four lines with deft fingers. The fish would be biting continuously and he would be kept busy cutting slivers of bait, pulling in bright-coloured parrot fish, herring and trevally, and throwing out again. Occasionally he would wipe a hand on his trousers and roll a cigarette from rich dark tobacco with a strong sweet smell.

When he had filled two boxes with little gleaming bait fish he would turn the sharp prow of *Shaleen* to the deep sea and the pulsing throb of the diesel would drive her out to where the sharks were. In the good times of the year his lines were set a long way out, and the land became a faint blue line on the sea-rim and often disappeared altogether. It was a lonely world out there, with no land in sight. The snowy-breasted albatrosses and giant black petrels brushed the wave-tops with their wings in long sweeps around the boat and *Shaleen* was a tiny speck in a great dark saucer of sea, with the wide sky and the wind-driven clouds above.

Sharkey saw strange things, in their seasons. The humpback whales rolled past on their spring and autumn migrations. The leather-backed Luth turtles, big as an upturned row-boat, occasionally sunned themselves saurian-fashion on the surface like something out of a vanished age of reptiles. Sperm whales with their bottle-heads, crooked spouts and squid-sucker scars on their shoulders sometimes came alongside. They had little eyes, surprisingly small in their vast bulk. Once he saw the giant squid, the kraken, itself. A vast brown formless thing in a wave trough, which looked at him with great liquid eyes and haunted him for a long time after in his sleep.

There were packs of dolphins, finning and tailing, whiskered sea lions far from shore, and once in a while a pod of killer whales following the humpbacks.

'Black an' white bastards!' Sharkey would grunt and spit. The killer whales were cruel in their harassment of the young whales, tearing at their mouths and tongues, and could wreck a deep-sea shark line out of sheer delight in destruction.

'There's a devil in 'em,' Sharkey said. He hated the killers, though he had a kindred feeling for most other things in the sea, even for the tiger sharks which were his great annoyance. Big tigers sometimes lived off his set-lines for weeks, taking fish every day close-bitten behind the gills or mangled for their livers. He caught tigers often enough, for most were not intelligent. Whalers, hammer-heads, and grey nurse, usually died on the line. But the tigers were always alive even after several days.

'Too mean to die', explained Sharkey. As the winch brought in the main line, the tigers would come up alongside the boat, grating their teeth on the hooks with their black eyes charcoal-red with hate.

'Watch the tail!' Sharkey would warn as the great striped bodies writhed and thrashed. 'Tail's as bad as the teeth on these sods . . .' And when you bent over with the gaff or tail-rope the shark's tail would crash against the side of the boat with blows which made the timbers shudder, the jaws snapping in anger and frustration at the planks which stood between us.

The sides of *Shaleen* where he usually gaffed the sharks were studded and scored with teeth marks. There were some teeth broken off in the hull and rudder and he would paint carefully around them on the annual refit. There is an old sea tradition that shark teeth are lucky.

46

Sharks were usually carried aft on the stern tray where the spray and wind kept them cool.

Once Sharkey found a straw beach hat inside a tiger shark and wore it round the boat.

His real name was Ted Nelson, and he was a big man with a pleasant brown face, faded blue eyes with weather lines around them, and thick knotted forearms. He was nearly sixty when I knew him but he looked much younger and was quick on his feet despite his broad-shouldered bulk. Usually he fished in bare feet. He said he liked to feel where he was stepping between the snouts and tails of the sharks on the blood-slippery deck.

'Put a foot wrong', he would say with a wink, 'and one of them bastards might snap you off at the knee'. Once a large carpet shark had reared up on a sunny deck five hours out of the water, and taken the seat and some of the underlying skin out of a crewhand's pants. 'Stopped 'im sitting down on the job for a week or two after', commented Ted with a chuckle.

He fished two to three kilometres of line depending on the time of season. Each set was marked by surface floats and wind-ragged flags on bamboo spears dipping on the swells. The main line lay along the sea bottom in the soft light forty or fifty metres down, with hooks running off it in short lines or snoods. Forty pound drags of lead placed at intervals kept it in position. When I called them anchors Ted corrected me.

47

'Not anchors. You never put an anchor on a sharkline. Give 'em something solid to tug against and they'll break the line like cotton. The drag is heavy enough to stop 'em travelling but light enough to give a bit. Once you get a few on the line they pull against each other.' His line was delicate and deadly as a spider's web.

Each of the hundreds of hooks was baited with a whole fish—parrot, herring, trevally, depending on season. The hooks and monel wire traces were surprisingly light. But they were set to catch the small bottom-feeding sharks which brought the best prices. It was intended that the big ones should straighten the hook or break away without damaging or tangling the main line.

School shark, a little bigger than a salmon, were highest-priced. They had a delicate white flesh and the buyers for fish shops filleted them into fine pieces and sold them as snapper, or cod, or even jewfish.

Whalers and grey nurse fetched fair prices until they were over two or three metres long. Ted was expert at reducing the size of a carcass with a big boning knife to make it look smaller. But it was hard to deceive the buyers at the morning auctions. They had educated noses and knowledgable prodding fingers which told them most things about a fish and its condition. There were no bruises on Ted's fish and he got top prices, though he usually preferred to sell direct to Vic. Paino. They had an understanding.

Tiger sharks brought no price at all. No one wanted the coarse, rough flesh and Sharkey would cut them off the line with an oath. If they were line robbers he would fire .22 bullets from a rifle with a cut-down barrel, the shots thudding into the hideous square heads until the eyes rolled white. 'Bastards never die!' he would grumble, torn between a grudging admiration of their toughness, and a resentment at the cost of the shells.

Sometimes he would cut out the great jaws with their razor crescent teeth and dry them for friends. Or if I were aboard he would run a knife down the full white bellies and open the stomach sacs. 'Looking for skindivers'. He regarded our underwater diving as only a partial degree this side of madness.

Like many men who make a living on the ocean he was careful never to go more than ankle-deep in it. 'I've seen too much of what swims, fins, crawls, and creeps in that old sea. The only shark that'll get me is the one that can squeeze through a bath tap.' And he would rumble with laughter at his own joke.

The tigers had all kinds of strange things in their stomachs. There were tins,

The tigers would come up alongside the boat grating their teeth on the hooks with their black eyes charcoal red with hate.

bottles, pieces of wood, old bones, dead dogs and cats washed out of the harbour, as well as dolphin skulls, bedraggled masses of feathers which had been albatrosses and cormorants. Even pieces of turtle shell and sea snakes which showed that some of them had come down from warmer northern waters.

'Real garbage gobblers, they are', said Ted. 'They'd eat your shadow if you gave 'em a chance.'

Once he found a straw hat inside a tiger and he wore it on the boat. And another time a woman's handbag with money and passport. He posted it to the address, and long afterwards received a brief note of thanks.

Despite the light hooks and traces he sometimes caught some tigers four metres long and more, their striped backs wider than a draught horse.

His hands were covered with scars. Once a tiger shark in a tangle of line had broken away from the side of the boat. One of the hooks in the fast running line flicked and caught Sharkey in the palm. The jerk of the shark drove the barb clean through the palm and out of the back of his hand

The whole weight of the line and the shark and the boat was on the hook through his hand. He played the shark for half an hour grimacing in agony. But he knew that if he weakened or let go his vice grip of the gunwhale with his other hand he would be overboard. And there could only be one end to that.

A doctor at Rottnest Island cut the hook out and wanted to send him to hospital. Ted thanked him politely, but said he had nine sharks to get to market, and drove his boat out of the bay with a bandaged hand.

Another scar on his right hand was from the needle teeth of a bronze whaler. When he reached overboard to shoot the three-metre shark it grabbed his hand and the rifle with a lightning sideways snap. Gasping with the pain he pulled his hand out of the maw—shredding it on the sharp teeth. The shark went to the bottom with the gun still gripped in its jaws. Ted wrapped his hand up in engine rags, and raised the shark with a crewhand. The shark was still holding the gun, and they tipped the water out of the barrel and found it still worked well enough to finish the troublesome whaler.

He always maintained that the stingray was the worst thing that ever happened to him. Hundreds got on the lines, and he used to flip them on their backs so they could not use the barbed sting in their tails, and cut the hooks out.

But on this day a big, sullen, black cowtail ray, with two eighteen centimetre barbs halfway down its tail flipped the right way up on a contrary wave and drove the stings deep into the junction of his thumb and hand. One of the tips broke off in the ball-socket of the thumb. He was blinded with agony and could not see. The hand swelled like an obscene blue sponge until only the tips of his fingers showed. He had morphine for two days, rolling and tossing, before the pain eased. Later it took a series of operations to remove the splintered pieces of barb from the joint.

But he still cuts rays off his line.

When the winch rumbled and the line came in, coil after dripping coil, you could sometimes tell by the change of noise when there was a shark on it. Often enough it would be seaweed, or a ray cupping its flat body against the pull. But sometimes there were huge beasts—tigers, or hammerheads with their gargoyle countenances, or deep-sea whalers with black-and-white mottled bellies and ragged fins. But the most magnificent of all were the rare great white sharks.

'They've got a big dark eye in that grim, grinning, pointed head. An eye as big as the palm of your hand. And they watch you every minute of the time. You can feel 'em looking at you. It sets the hairs up on the back of your neck, I'll tell you!'

The whites, sometimes called 'white pointers' or 'white deaths', were the kings. Immense creatures so much bigger, stronger and more predatory than the whalers, grey nurse, and common sharks. They were like the lion to the jungle jackal. Individuals longer than nine metres have been caught, but bigger ones are believed to exist. In prehistoric times monsters of twenty-four and twenty-seven metres swam the oceans and their teeth come up from time to time in fishing boat trawls and dredges. It may be that they are not entirely extinct.

The great whites commonly encountered on the Australian coast run from 3.6 to six metres and at this size are formidable beasts. They live on seals and tuna, porpoises, sick whales, and large prey and they are equipped accordingly with teeth which can cut through meat and bone like a mechanical saw.

Fortunately for swimmers they are a deep-sea shark, seldom coming into shallow water. The ones Sharkey hooked from time to time looked so immense that the imagination could not cope with the thought of a beast twice the size. The five-metre whites were already as heavy as two bullocks. They could move at forty-eight km/h, turn in their own length, and bite a twenty-three litre chunk of blubber out of the tough hide of a dead sperm whale. Leaping out of the water to clamp on to the whale's flank they would hang on by their teeth, shaking and worrying until the immense piece of flesh tore away in their jaws.

'They never shut their mouths entirely', said Ted. 'They can't. The top teeth lie back flat in three rows when they want them to. But the bottom teeth always stand up. Like spears. Those are the teeth, you see, that they strike with when they make a charge.'

The teeth were triangular and five centimetres long with serrated edges sharper than knives, each spaced behind the other in rows. When one was damaged another came forward to take its place.

Ted would set himself for the battle with an eagerness and delight that was in contrast to his usual calm. He saw the big sharks as a challenge. It was like catching a kingfish on a cotton reel. One kick of the spade tail, one swirl or lunge, and the hook would straighten or the line break and he lost far more whites than he brought in. Watching him play one was a sight in itself.

'Steady, steady!' Ted would breathe, balanced delicately on the balls of his feet, working the great shark gently up to the surface. 'Tug hard and he'll straighten the hook.' He would feel the weight carefully through the tight trembling line. 'Gently does it . . .'

'Ah, there he goes!' and the wet sisal rope would rush out over the gunwhale as the fish made a run. Loop after loop of line flicking up off the deck and disappearing overboard, hissing through his hands as he kept the tension on the line.

Patiently Ted would let the shark run. Deep, deep, down into the blue depths, the angry beat of the great tail coming back through the line and telltaling all its movements.

'He's a big fish. A beauty. If he knew his own strength we'd never hold him. But we'll try, boy, we'll try!'

And he would turn the shark gently at the end of its run and patiently work it up to the surface again, until the huge grey bulk began to appear, an enormous shadow with huge wing-like pectoral fins below the boat where the light rays slanted down into the depths.

'That's the time, Hughie. When we get 'em or we lose 'em. The moment of truth of it all, you might say.'

With the great sharks alongside the boat there was a chance to get a big gaff

50

into the gills, a rope around the tail so that it could be contained in impotent lashing and bloody froth. Huge jaws crashing, and the dark eye rolling in the knowledge of imminent defeat.

But it was also the moment when the sharks could most easily be lost. That moment when they saw the boat and the man. The eye was always watching, as Ted had said. At the first movement of the gaff or the tail rope they were likely to snatch and break the light line and roll away to freedom in a swirl that showed their huge white bellies.

Often enough they did, and afterwards Ted did not seem to mind very much. 'Now there was a fish! What a beauty that one was!'

When he did catch them, and the gaff was in and the spade tail was lashed impotently to the stern bollard, when the bullets had thudded into the broad head, and life and intelligence and hate had faded from the huge dark eye, he was quiet and thoughtful. Not jubilant or triumphant as you might expect.

The long tow to port would begin. The big sharks were rarely caught, and often he got a good price for them for exhibition. They would be loaded on a truck by a wharf crane, and people would pay to come and gasp at their size, and run a finger over the teeth, and shiver deliciously that they were not in the sea with THAT coming after them.

Ted never went to the exhibitions. When I mentioned them once he spat. There was something between him and the shark which was sullied by the exhibition of the bloated corpse. It was the catching which was the challenge to him, and he often spoke of hooking something really big, with a line made to hold huge fish. Not his light commercial line.

'There are sharks out there bigger'n anyone's ever dreamed of', he would say. 'One day, Hughie, you an' me we'll go out and we'll take a real big set. Hooks to hold a bull sperm whale, and a line that'll tear the bottom up out of the ocean. When we pull the fish up out of that black water he'll be bigger than the boat. You'll see.'

But we did not catch the shark. Ted died that summer. Not as he would have preferred, by the sea, or a great wave, or a shark, but by the crab. Cancer.

I have often wondered since what it would have been like out there, out of sight of land, fast to the ultimate shark, Sharkey taking the strain with his back and knotted forearms, and saying 'Steady, steady-oh!' to himself, and the line quivering down, taut as a piano wire into the depths where the enormous shadow moved far below our keel . . .

51

H.M.A.S. PERTH
SUNK DURING THE BATTLE OF SUNDA STRAIT
IN MARCH 1942
THIS 4 INCH SHELL CASE WAS RECOVERED FROM THE SHIP
BY
DAVE BURCHELL
AND PRESENTED TO
THE CITY OF PERTH
JULY 1967

At the Bottom of Sunda Strait: HMAS *Perth*

DAVE BURCHELL

HMAS Perth was a 6,800-ton light cruiser of the Royal Australian Navy. Her ship's company was 682 officers and men, and in 1942—after distinguished service in the Mediterranean against the Axis powers—she was sent to face the Japanese in the Java Sea. *Perth* was sailing into a trap from which she would never escape.

The *Repulse* and the *Prince of Wales*, pride of the Royal Navy, were sunk off Malaya. Twelve of the fourteen remaining Allied ships, British, Dutch and American, were sunk in the disastrous Battle of the Java Sea. Only HMAS *Perth* and USS *Houston* remained. It was vital that they gain the safety of the open Indian Ocean, and the way to freedom lay through the narrow gate of Sunda Strait.

On February 28th, 1942, the two ships made the break in darkness to avoid enemy aircraft. But by cruel ill-chance they ran headlong into an enemy invasion fleet off Point St. Nicolas within a few short miles of freedom.

Perth took the first onslaught, lasting just over an hour. At the finish she had used all her ammunition and, sinking and burning, was firing star shells and practice bricks. *Houston* lasted a little longer, and was reduced to firing .50 calibre machine gun bullets when her own ammunition ran out. Though they inflicted enormous casualties among the close-packed invasion fleet, the issue was never in doubt. The two ships went down amid a hail of torpedo and shell fire.

Dave Burchell, who conceived the idea of locating the missing and heroic HMAS *Perth* in 1967, lost a leg in a rail accident at the age of 16. Since then he has successively been a stunt high-tower diver, an author, president of North Adelaide Football Club, and probably South Australia's best known underwater diver. He once jumped by parachute in full diving gear from 670 m into St Vincent's Gulf to rendezvous with a submarine fifteen metres down, just to prove it could be done.

Sometimes you have a a premonition. A feeling deep down that something important is about to happen.

The adrenalin surges, the muscles tense, and you find reserves of endurance that astonish you when you think about it all later on—well, sometimes!

On the afternoon of what was probably the greatest diving experience of my life there was no faster heartbeat of anticipation. In fact it was an opposite

Laying a wreath over the grave of the *Perth* at the conclusion of the dives.

The wreath over the dead ship. Strangely the currents ran fiercely every day, but when the wreath was laid it was an unusual time of slack water and it hovered over the wreck a long time. The red flag is one of the wreck markers.

situation. Aboard our Indonesian Navy vessel, a Russian-built sloop named the *Aires* (which had dragged herself unwillingly to sea after three years on a mud-bank) I felt flat, dejected, and ready to quit.

As I was lying on a mattress on the foredeck of the *Aires* puffing disconsolately on a clove-scented Indonesian cigarette, Sumantri sat beside me. He took in my dejected expression at a glance.

'Well, Daddy', he said—he called me that since he'd seen one of the kid's letters. 'The fishermen say they have another big ship for you. About three miles to the east.'

'Probably just another Jap. Haven't they got anything further west?'

I'd just dived sixty metres to a dead Japanese troop carrier, and though it was intensely interesting, the bottom of Sunda Strait was a long way to go for the wrong ship.

Now the Indonesian fishermen Salim and Makri in their dugout canoes had snagged another ship to the east. It was about eleven kilometres from where the Navy figured the *Perth* had gone down and I honestly believed it would be a waste of time. 'You're sure there's nothing else?'

Sumantri shook his head. 'That's all they seem to know of.'

I knew the wreck had to be checked, if only to keep the fishermen interested and to keep faith with Sumantri of the Indonesian Navy who had given so much help. Diving searches are also often a slow and tiresome process of elimination, and the slogging has to be done.

'OK' I replied. 'Let's have a look.'

It began badly. The fishermen had snagged the wreck with a weight and their nylon line. When I got in the water already soaked in sweat inside my wetsuit (necessary because of jellyfish), superheated and darned uncomfortable, the line felt thin and slippery as wire. A nine km/h current was running and try as I would I couldn't even pull myself below the surface.

Instead I floundered around for a minute or two looking ridiculous, feeling worse, and using up air. Then I hauled myself up and flopped winded on the dinghy.

'Too much current', said John Scammell, my tender, concerned. 'Let's give it away for the day.'

Privately I agreed with him. But perhaps the fact that I disliked the dive so much was what made me all the more determined to go on with it.

Of course it was all wrong technically. I had spent years instructing divers on the dangers of solo swimming, particularly on deep dives. Now here I was breaking all the rules.

'Let's try it with a thicker line', I suggested to the ever-patient John. 'Something I can hang on to.'

He gave me a resigned look and at that moment the light line broke under the weight of the dinghy, and we went spinning off down Sunda Strait on the current. *Aires* had to come and rescue us and tow us back. Very ignominious.

By the time we arrived back over the wreck everyone was pretty sick of the deal, but I badgered my good friend Sumantri into asking the fishermen to try again as I was anxious to identify the 'Jap' so that we could leave it and work more to the west.

After some trouble manoeuvring, the fishermen again hooked the wreck. this time using a one and a quarter centimetre-diameter rope and a four and a half kilogram shot. The day was very hot, and even underwater it wasn't much better, for the sea was warm and thick, with the porridge-like plankton sticking to the rope, making it slippery against my rubber gloves. But by sheer persistance I managed to make some progress down the line.

At about forty-five metres the school fish started to appear, and I knew I was nearly there.

For a while there was nothing. Then from out of the grey mist a ship started to take shape under me. At first it was just a confused pattern of steel plates and rivets, but the visibility was improving, now more than six metres, which was really something for Sunda Strait, and I could make out the shape of a propeller with the rope leading straight to it. This was better than I'd hoped, for once on the propeller it should be easy enough to find hand-holds to work back to the hull. Props were also good for identification.

After a lot of battling against the current I stood up on the drive shaft and inspected the propeller. It was larger than the one on the freighter we'd found that morning, with the blades more clover shaped. Taking hold of the edge I peered out into the current, immediately springing back, in my haste almost losing my footing. There was a shark pack gliding along in line astern making straight for me!

Pressing back against the blade of the propeller I watched the sharks as they circled, counting them. There were six, and each one looked lean and fast and

Entering up the diving log with John Scammell.

had cold swivelling eyes. I reckoned that I was safe enough where I was. But I couldn't stay there. The only escape from the sharks seemed to be the rope, stretching away into the fog across the hull. It looked awfully open and unprotected, and after first checking my air supply, I looked quickly around for possible alternatives.

It was then, almost at the limit of visibility, that I saw the second propeller. I experienced a chill far more sudden and severe than that brought on by the sight of the sharks. This was no freighter! Twin propellers on the starboard side could mean only one thing . . . this was a four-screw ship, a warship, and the only warships in the area were the *Perth* and *Houston*.

Was it the *Perth*? It seemed too good to be true. I had to know the answer. A check of my air supply and instruments showed I had another ten minutes. With luck there was time.

There was still the shark pack, but I had renewed determination. To reach the hull I had to cover three metres or so of open water. Waiting for a break in their picket line I leapt across. Unfortunately, one of the sharks had got out of sequence in its circling, and as I sprang from behind the protection of the blade we very nearly collided. My karate-like yell was a hundred per cent fright, despite my new-found courage, but it served its purpose and the shark nearly turned inside-out in its effort to avoid contact.

After that they all vanished leaving me on the aft deck of a vessel canted over to port. Peering through the porridge-warm sea, misty with sediment, I looked up and for the third time that day was stopped in my tracks. I saw a gun turret with twin barrels like two dark shadows above my head.

I knew that the USS *Houston* sunk on the same night as the *Perth* had triple guns in her turrets. *Perth* was the one with twin guns. Twin six-inch guns . . .

Working along the rail to give myself leeway I swam hard across the current and rugby-tackled a gun barrel as I was swept past. The bore was nearly choked with coral and as I looked inside a small blue fish popped out. Measuring the bore with my hand confirmed it. A six-inch bore—we had found the *Perth*!

After the celebrations and the excitement of finding her I realised, of course, that there was more to it than just one bounce-dive. After all I had only seen a fraction of a vessel that was 169 m long, sixteen metres in the beam, and stood thirty metres off the seabed—even canted over as she was.

Altogether I made thirty dives on the *Perth*. First we placed buoys at thirty-metre intervals, and I'd dive and survey that area. Then move on to the next.

I soon found what must have been her mortal wound, inflicted by a torpedo, or perhaps a pair of 'tin-fish' fired together, for deep in the starboard side of her hull, approximately under A turret, there was a gaping hole about twelve metres across. But the rest of her visible side was undamaged, with even most of the glass still intact in the scuttles. Despite twenty-five years the *Perth* was the most perfect wreck I have ever seen. Up forward, her anchors were in place, and the characteristic cruiser bow still swept down in one clean unbroken line.

On the four-inch gun deck the barrels pointed in all directions, with S2 turret at least having received a direct hit, as several live rounds, bent at right angles, were lying inside.

The port torpedo quad was under the ship, and I couldn't reach it, but on the starboard side the four tubes were empty with the muzzles slightly trained out, and in some of the places I rubbed with my glove, the brass work was still shiny under the thin film of calcified marine growth that covered it.

On the deck near the aft control was a vehicle that I first took to be a truck, but which turned out to be some sort of fire-fighting unit. I inspected its tyres; they were Dunlops and still seemed to be inflated.

On the upper bridge where Captain Hec Waller and his senior officers had been killed by a salvo of shells just after he gave the order 'Abandon Ship!', the damage was more evident. The standard compass and most of the other navigational instruments were gone and there were several shell holes in the deck.

Along the front of the bridge the groups of voice tubes showed shrapnel damage but the row of stainless steel handles for winding up the weather screens were untouched, and glinted dully through the grey green water.

The bridge held a strong fascination for me, and I never tired of spending time there visualising the scenes that must have taken place on it. Particularly that final night when *Perth* went to her end caught in the web of Japanese searchlights and shell fire.

On the starboard side of the bridge, growing from out of the guard rail and defying the current, was a magnificent spray of gorgonia coral. It was over two metres across and because of the depth it looked grey in colour, but in fact was probably orange or dark red. I was always careful not to damage it. The ship is still there, with the mortal remains of the men she took down with her,

Cleaning up relics; the binnacle on the *Aires'* deck.

Western Australian survivors of the *Perth*'s sinking inspect the relics from Sunda Strait. Burchell has gyro-compass repeater in hand.

and I feel the coral spray represents a living tribute to the memory of both the ship and the men.

After the survey dives were completed we began a serious search for the bell. But this was to be a disappointment. It was in the quartermaster's lobby on the underside of the ship, and there was just no way of getting through to it.

During the thirty dives I made on the *Perth* I recovered some twenty-four different relics. These included shell cases from the four-inch gun turrets, navigational instruments, and a signalling light from the bridge, voice tubes and gyro repeaters from the wheelhouse, and other miscellaneous pieces from different areas.

Some came easily, and these I was mostly able to carry up with me. Some were more difficult to recover. The signalling light from the bridge probably caused us the most trouble. I had seen it on several occasions; it was about the size of a fifty-six litre drum, and looked as if it would be heavy and awkward to handle.

Lying half out of its mounts with one of its octagonal panes of glass broken,

the light also had a large hole in its side, indicating that it had been hit by shell fire. It took a whole dive to clear it completely from the ship, and the rope slipped and we nearly lost it on the way up.

The four-inch shell cases didn't present anywhere near the problem of the signal light in the way of weight, though there was the question of sensitivity of the explosives. They were mostly recovered from S2, the starboard aft turret, about twelve metres up from the sea-bed.

The first time I looked inside, I could see a number of empty shell cases and several live rounds in a heap on the deck. Two of the live rounds were bent at right angles, again the evidence of a direct hit.

Thinking that Gordon Reid, the President of the Ex-*Perth* Association, would like a shell case, as he had been a four-inch gunner, I moved in to pick one up, only to find that they were all fused together with calcified marine growth. However, as I had my pick hammer with me I sat down in the turret and started the delicate job of chipping the shells apart. I knew it was highly unlikely that one of the live rounds would explode, although it did cross my mind, I'll admit.

From inside the wheelhouse I recovered a beautiful copper voice tube mouthpiece on the inside of which was an engraved brass plate reading 'No. 44. Upper Bridge Starboard'. Also in the wheelhouse was a bronze gyro-compass repeater. It was extremely heavy and wrung complaints from Scammell and the crew hauling up in the dinghy above.

An item which looked like a hard-hat diver's helmet in the debris of the bridge turned out to be one of the most exciting finds of all. The compass binnacle.

All too soon it was time to go. It had been too brief a time, but there were many things I would never forget.

One of them was when I went to pay the Javanese fishermen Salim and Makri who had located the wrecks. To my astonishment they refused.

Sumantri, my liaison officer with the Indonesian Navy, translated for me. 'They say you have worked so hard on this they don't want any money. They want to be part of it, and their headman ashore agrees.'

I was flabbergasted. The sum involved, paltry enough to us, was an entire year's earnings to these men.

Naturally I insisted on the payment. But I was so impressed by their attitude that we gave them a real send-off, dressing ship, making a speech and making them both honorary members of the Underwater Explorers Club of South

Thanking the Indonesian fishermen Salim and Makri and making them members of the Underwater Explorers Club of South Australia.

Burchell hands over voice tube mouthpiece of old HMAS *Perth* to Captain David Leach, commander of the new HMAS *Perth*.

Australia. We also gave them food and medical supplies and our sincere gratitude. As well as the fishermen I could never thank Sumantri enough for all he had done.

The relics weighed about 270 kg overall and we had some trouble getting them back to Australia. I was hopeful that Qantas, our national airline, would fly them back, but strangely they refused. In the end the *Perth Sunday Times*, Channel 9 in Western Australia, and Malayan Singapore Airlines organised the lift.

It was touching to see how the survivors of the *Perth* in various States reacted to seeing portions of their old ship again. They obviously meant a great deal to them—more than I could have imagined.

The various pieces were distributed around. The City of Perth had one of the HMAS *Perth* shell casings, suitably mounted. A porthole rim went to the Perth Memorial Hall at the RAN shore-base in Fremantle. The Ex-Navalmen's Association in Adelaide has a part of a navigational instrument from the bridge. John Scammell and Gordon Reid had shell casings, and I kept a voice tube. Another voice-tube mouthpiece was presented to the Navy and incorporated on the bridge of the new HMAS *Perth*, which I thought was rather appropriate.

The binnacle and the larger relics were officially handed over to the Chief of Naval Staff, Admiral Sir Alan McNichol, on Remembrance Day, 1967, for the Australian War Memorial at Canberra.

The little brass lampholder from the compass binnacle went to a special destination. Captain Hector Waller must have been standing close to it when he died. Now Mrs Waller has the lampholder. She lights a candle in it each Christmas Eve and the bright flame is a silent memory to Captain Waller, his men and his ship.

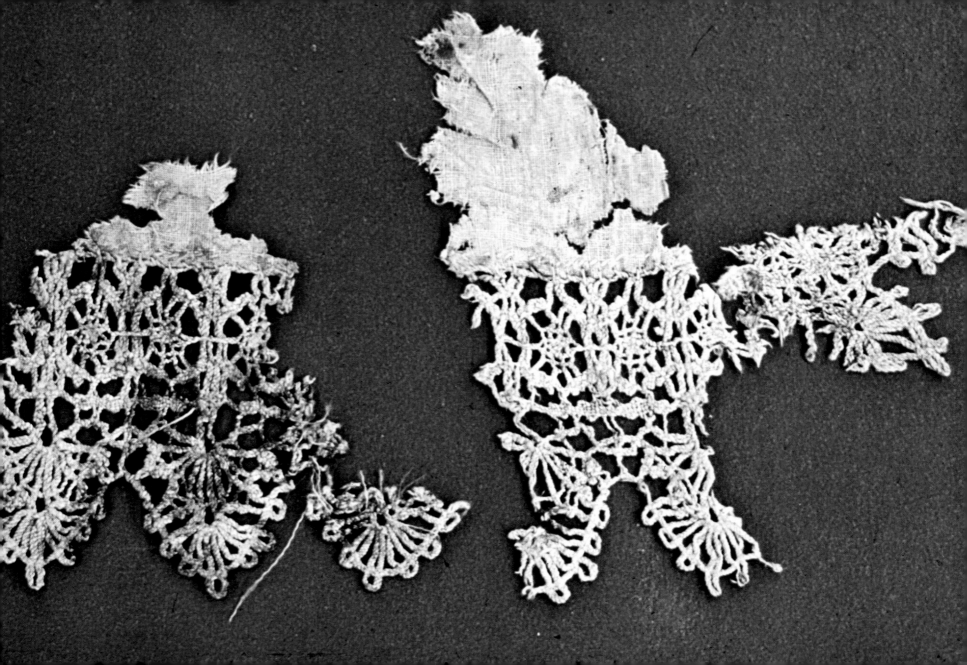

A
Fragment
of Lace

MARILYN EDWARDS

In 1629 the Dutch East India Company fleet-flagship *Batavia*, on her way to the Spice Islands, sailed too far on her easterly course and was wrecked on the low coral islands of the Abrolhos, seventy-two kilometres off the Western Australian coast.

She had treasure aboard—twelve chests of coin, jewels, silverware, cameos, as well as 316 men, women and children. Long before she entered Australian waters plotters, led by Jeronimus Cornelisz, had schemed to kill the fleet President Francisco Pelsaert, throw his body to the sharks, and sail for the Barbary coast with the treasure.

The wreck, altered, but did not entirely change, their plans. Pelsaert and the officers sailed for Java 2400 kilometres away to get help from the nearest Dutch settlement. They departed in a manner more hasty than dignified, leaving themselves open to the accusation of abandoning the people and the wreck. Unintentionally they also left the people to the wolf-pack mutineers, who planned to murder most of them and seize the rescue ship.

They killed 125 men, women and children, some of them in the most frightful fashion. Pelsaert returned months later with the rescue ship too late to prevent the massacres but in time to torture and execute the mutineer ringleaders in grisly fashion. He also salvaged ten of the twelve chests of treasure from the sunken wreck with native divers from Gujerat.

Lost for many years, the wreck was located in the 1960s off Morning Reef in the Wallabi Islands of the Abrolhos.

Hugh Edwards was involved in the early research and diving during the 1960s, and in 1970 he led an expedition to the wreck in which his wife Marilyn —also a diver and writer—played an important part.

'Silver!' The cry rang out across the water, and a diver heaved himself over the edge of the boat spilling a bag full of coral-encrusted coins.

They clattered down with the unmistakable ring of ancient precious metal, and the diver—my husband Hugh, dripping streams of water from his black wetsuit into the boat—pushed his mask back, picked one up and turned it over in his hand. He whistled.

'Look at this!' he said, rubbing at the encrustation. I could see a floral cross, and what looked like a date.

'Fifteen sixty eight', Hugh said. 'This coin was minted twenty years before the Spanish Armada sailed!'

'Are there many more like that?' I asked. He nodded briefly. 'The bottom's littered with them.' Then he was gone again, leaving me in the boat tossing with a motion I never quite got used to. Me and the treasure.

It was funny, I thought, that whenever people talked of wrecks and treasure it conjured illusions of the Caribbean, Mexico, or the Mediterranean. Yet here we were off our own Western Australian coast, diving on a treasure worth at least the ransom of one of the princes whose heads were stamped on the backs of the coins—Johan of Denmark, William of Orange, Frederick, Gottfried, Augustus, Maximilian, and others, with their armour and cold eyes.

The heads were interesting, from a woman's point of view. The faces were strong, harsh, with the arrogant expression of men who ruled by the sword and held men's lives in their hands.

They were men dead 350 years and more. Men who had never heard of Australia—the land at the bottom of the world where their faces finished up looking at the surface from under three fathoms of green water.

Their own world was displayed in their coats of arms—jousting lances, armour, shields, maces, stags, lions, griffins, and heraldic designs of a Europe still in the grip of the Middle Ages.

'You'll like this better', Hugh said, reappearing, taking out his mouthpiece and passing a handful of tiny things that tinkled and gleamed over the side of the boat.

They were hooks and eyes from a woman's dress of long ago. And pins—long brass pins with large spherical heads—all unmistakably feminine.

'Found the vanity box', he said with a wink, and disappeared again in a cascading stream of bubbles to become a black shadow in the depths again.

He knew my mind. The coins were fascinating. There was no doubt about that, and the men themselves never tired of them. But to me the real treasure lay in the little personal things in the wreck. The hooks-and-eyes, for instance, were just like the ones on my own dresses (left behind in the wardrobe at home, for the Abrolhos are strictly jeans territory). But I could just imagine one of the Dutch women passengers standing in front of a propped-up mirror on the ship and hooking them up, or doing her long hair with one of the ivory combs we found in the wreck for a special dinner or formal occasion as the ship rolled along her course.

The *Batavia* women had such a terrible time, I remembered—murdered cruelly by the mutineers or forced into prostitution under the threat of death.

Perhaps the dress belonged to the beautiful Lucretia Jansz whom all men desired, according to the ancient story.

The mutineer ringleader, the mad Jeronimus Cornelisz, kept Lucretia Jansz prisoner in his tent. It was recorded in the dry matter-of-fact way of official documents that he had—out of his colossal conceit—tried to win her, imagining that his charm and persuasion could put the killings and torture and her absent husband Boudewyn out of her mind.

Wreck-jewellery; bracelet of pieces-of-eight, dolphin ring from wreck silver, ring with piece-of-two, and ring incorporating a sapphire from the camp of the *Zeewyk* survivors. (M. Edwards) ▼

Barber's bowls, tortoiseshell comb, unguent jars, and pipe. Note the indentation for 'cupping' (as it was called) against a vein in arm or leg, or tucking under the chin for shaving. (WA Museum) ►

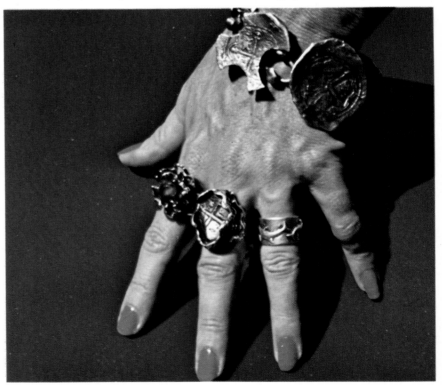

She resisted him twelve days, in the tent hung with the richest of the cloths and trappings salvaged from the wreck on nearby Morning Reef. On the thirteenth day David Seevanck, a monster even among the unprincipled scoundrels following Cornelisz, told her discreetly that if she did not please the Captain General (a title Cornelisz had assumed) she would have her throat cut 'Like the other women' . . . the ugly, pure, and pregnant ones. She knew he meant it and gave in that day.

For Lucretia and the others, life on the Abrolhos must have been a hell. The bright stars, and the sunsets, the blue smiling waters, a seeming mockery, in a trap from which they might never escape, with death a daily event.

In fact, Lucretia, who was desired by Cornelisz, by Ariaen Jacobsz the skipper of the *Batavia*, and probably by Francisco Pelsaert the president of the fleet himself, lived through it all and did escape when the rescue ship came.

She found herself a widow, to add to her shame at Cornelisz' hands. For her husband Boudewyn, who had gone out to the East Indies before her, had died meantime in the tropics. So much sorrow in so short a time.

On one day's diving after we had finished photographing the site, Hugh and Neville Willsea tied lifting lines around some huge pieces of conglomerate on the bottom which had broken away and were in danger of erosion.

They had a difficult time raising them, even though Neville is red-headed and as strong as a bull. But when they brought them ashore the conglomerate was a mass of interesting objects welded together with pitch, sand and coral, all

set like cement which cracked and crumbled when brought ashore.

Among the relics were two pieces which looked like those dish-like British steel helmets from the two world wars or Dad's Army. Except that each had an indentation, a semi-circular bite out of the rim.

'Tin hats', Hugh said jokingly, adding, 'Of course, they can't be. What do you suppose they really are?'

'Moorish fruit bowls?' I suggested, knowing that Pelsaert had lost some silver dishes in the wreck.

'Could be', he said doubtfully, not really convinced.

It was some days later that Max Cramer came to visit us. He tucked one into his neck and said, 'Aha! Soup bowls for sloppy soup eaters!'

'Or maybe shaving bowls?' I said. 'See how the indentation fits your throat.'

'I think you're right', Max said with surprise, and we were right. The bowls' indentations fitted neatly under the chin. They *were* barber's bowls, and they had even more significance than that, as we discovered later.

The barber's bowls on the *Batavia* belonged to Maistre Fransz Jansz of Hoorn. Like other members of his profession in those times he was also a surgeon and was officially entered as barber-surgeon on lists of the ship's company. The fact that he was a senior man aboard is shown by the courtesy title 'Maistre', Master, or Mister, and his high listing in the roll of the 316 men, women and children aboard.

Apart from trimming beards and moustaches and shaving customers, a barber-surgeon of seventeenth century Europe was usually an expert in blood-letting, for bleeding had been a common remedy recommended for all kinds of illnesses and ailments for hundreds of years.

The indentations in our barber's bowls, we discovered, were not just for shaving. Though they were very handy for that. But they were also for 'cupping', or placing the bowl against vein pressure points in arms or legs. A tourniquet was applied, the area was warmed, massaged, rubbed with ointment, then lightly pierced with a sharp (and probably none-too-clean) instrument.

Up to two pints of blood were taken at a time to relieve imagined 'humours' in cupping bowls. Though medical journals of the time warned that 'blood letting, like wine drinking, is right enough in moderation. But an excess leads to disaster', disasters occurred often enough. They included blood poisoning from dirty instruments, for sterilisation was unknown.

Marilyn diving on a 1629 *Batavia* cannon.
Sailor's clay pipe. ◄

A ducaton. ▲
Pots, candlesticks, coins, jugs. ►

Some patients were literally bled to death by their barber-surgeons. Researching on our barber's bowls I found that blood-letting was the origin of the traditional barber's sign, a red-and-white striped pole outside the shop. I wonder how many modern barbers know THAT?

Inside the cupping bowls in a mass of conglomerate were unguent and ointment jars for the bleeding, the remains of towels, and ivory combs—Maistre Jansz' professional equipment.

After the meeting the barber was one of the folk enslaved in the service of the

mutineers, and forced to attend the arch-villain Jeronimus Cornelisz. Cornelisz tired of him soon enough. Like all men who come to power by subterfuge he was wary and suspicious of counter plots, and he feared that Jansz might become an informer.

'Kill him!' he said to his lieutenants.

Under the pretence that they were going hunting seals they took him to East Wallabi Island, a high scrub-covered bluff overlooking the modern crayfishing anchorage of Pigeon Island.

Poor Fransz Jansz. On the barren slopes of East Wallabi where he died eagles soar today, and for three centuries—long after his bleached bones crumbled and became part of the earth—his bleeding bowls lay in the wreck to be found in 1970 by our expedition.

Not all the skeletons were left in the open. Some were buried and were found, complete with sword hacks and other marks of violent death, in the 1960s on the little coral cay called Beacon Island today, but known to the old Dutch by the singularly apt name of 'Bataviae's Kerkhoff'—Batavia's Graveyard.

On our 1970 expedition Neville Willsea had a terrible nightmare that a skeleton arm was coming under the tent flap and plucking at him. 'I've never had such a realistic dream', he said, still pale at the memory. It was likely that people had been murdered on our island and I said 'Why don't you dig and see if there's really a skeleton there?'

'Not on your life', he said, shaking his head with great emphasis.

'But why not?' I asked.

'Well I don't believe in ghosts, and if there really was a skeleton there I'd never sleep a wink again.'

The mutineers' victims were avenged. The *Batavia* story reads like a Shakespearian play. Pelsaert, who left in one of the ship's boats to seek help (the passengers claimed he had gone to save his own skin), returned to find a small group of loyalists desperately defending themselves on West Wallabi Island.

The villains were forced to surrender, tortured until they confessed (regular legal procedure at the time) and then tried on the basis of their confessions. The detailed accounts of their crimes on the islands make ghastly reading even today. They behaved more like animals than men.

The justice meted out to them was severe in proportion. Cornelisz and the

In red suit with candlestick and spoon. ▲   Marilyn and wreck-pottery.

ring leaders were hanged after having hands cut off. Others were taken to the Dutch city of Batavia (modern Djakarta) in the East Indies and were executed there, one man by the horrific mediaeval death of breaking on the wheel.

So much blood, violence, and death, for the money, the treasure, that the ship *Batavia* had carried.

Perhaps that is one reason why I never felt the same way about the salvaged coin, the symbols of sorrow, that I did about the other relics, the personal momentoes of people who lived and walked and breathed the Abrolhos air three centuries ago.

Often I would walk out of our tent and imagine how it must have been for them. Reading through Henrietta Drake Brockman's books and research and the translations of the old documents, the story was a very human one. Despite the coldness of the official reports you began to feel you knew the people concerned, and I would wonder as I wrote down the day's diving haul from the wreck who the various items had belonged to.

Mostly it was pure speculation—guessing—though I used to claim feminine intuition, which made the divers laugh and say rude things about feminine illogic. It is considered very wicked, in historical circles, to jump to conclusions without solid facts to work on.

But when you find something like, say, our sections of ceremonial armour or the fragment of lace it is impossible (or inhuman) not to wonder who wore it, long ago.

The armour was rich and ceremonial with gold gilt on the studs and an embossed pattern. When Hugh found it by accident after a winter storm had opened up a part of the wreck, the leather backing was still soft and supple, and though the iron was chemically changed, the shapes of the breast-plate, the neck and arm joints were still there. It looked like the armour worn by the princes on the coins.

Did it belong to Pelsaert? As a sophisticated merchant I couldn't quite picture him in it, though a metal breast-plate was an uncomfortable part of official formal dress in those days. Perhaps it was for the Governor Jan Pieterszoon Coen in the East Indies, or some other distinguished and military personage. Or perhaps it was one of Pelsaert's gifts for eastern princes along with silver bowls and flagons, a silver bedstead, jewels and cameos.

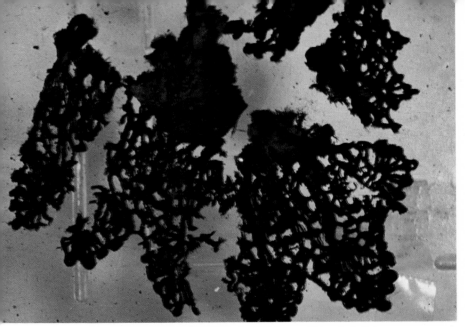

▲The lace as it uncurled from the con-glomerate. (Photo C. Pearson, WA Museum)

The lace after preservative treatment in Dr Pearson's laboratory. (Photo C. Pearson)

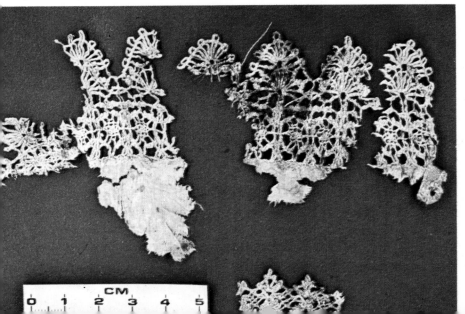

The lace was another thing. It appeared in the conglomerate—a black concrete-like mass with pottery, brass objects, and other things cemented inside it—as just a grubby piece of string. The men looked at it without interest.

But something about it caught my eye. I picked it up and unravelled it patiently, and there it was—a fragment of lace—blackened and discoloured certainly, but astonishingly preserved after all the years—Italian bobbin lace.

I remembered the pictures of Rembrandt, of wealthy Dutch men and women of the *Batavia*'s time, dressed in rich black velvet with bunches of such lace at their throats, and their cuffs, a mark of gentility and prosperity.

Pelsaert—the senior merchant? Could the lace have been worn at his throat or cuff? Or could it have come from the luggage of Lucretia Jansz, the only woman aboard the *Batavia* wealthy enough to have a maidservant accompany her on the voyage?

For Pelsaert the *Batavia* affair ended badly. He was accused of deserting the people on the islands, leaving them to the mercy of the mutineers with no senior Company men to enforce order or discipline. There was no need for him to have gone with the ship's boats, it was said, when he could have sent the sailors instead and remained himself to keep firm command.

After the wreck, and the horror of discovering the mutiny and the savage but necessary (according to the thinking of the time) reprisals, he was a broken man in health and his career was in ruins. He died in the East Indies a year after the wreck. The Company confiscated his wages and possessions.

Lucretia lived to become an old, old lady. She married again in the East Indies. When her second husband died she married a third time. Obviously her attractions were not diminished by her Abrolhos' experiences. Though she had no children of her own, she was godmother to several. Since this was an important honour in Holland, it seems that people did not hold the shame of the Abrolhos against her and thought her more sinned against than sinner.

She lived a long and full life, and died in Amsterdam, perhaps the last of the *Batavia* people.

History has never appealed to me in terms of battles or dates, and I don't especially care for it as expressed in wreck silver. But a hook-and-eye and a fragment of lace made a part of early Dutch Australian history come very much alive for me. History you could touch and feel.

67

Riding
the
Whale Shark

BEN CROPP

Winner of the 1953 Australian Open Spearfishing Championship, and the national senior title in 1961. With his enterprising approach to diving it was inevitable that he should look for further challenge, and he left his profession of school-teaching to become a full-time diver and underwater cameraman early in the 1960s.

He was almost immediately successful—despite the advice of surface photographic experts that it would take him five years to learn how to handle a motion picture camera to professional standards. Within a few months he was producing his own documentary films on sharks, and in 1964 he won the U.S. Underwater Photographer of the Year award, and sold a number of television films to American networks to make the first break-through for Australian diving productions overseas. He has followed this early success with regular Ben Cropp specials on diving and marine life.

Though his first films were on spearfishing and killing sharks, and there was a temptation to continue a successful theme, Cropp put his speargun away early in the piece and became one of the early conservationists. Today his films on the Australian coast, Coral Sea, and Great Barrier Reef, are regularly exported to Japan, America, and Europe. But there was a time when it seemed his decision to film only living creatures might have reacted against him.

On a Sunday night in February 1965, I was sitting at home in Collaroy brooding over my cancelled U.S. film promotion trip.

I had been booked to fly the following day. On my last American visit I'd sold three shark films—*Shark Hunters*, *Shark Safari*, and *Challenge of the Sea* to the big NBC and ABC colour TV networks, and the prospects for further sales were good.

But this time my offering was a series of films on taming fish and marine animals, which to my self-critical eye were short on action. At the last moment I lost confidence. It seemed to me that the films all lacked dramatic action, a climax. If I didn't believe in them myself how could I hope to sell them?

I worried about it for weeks, and at the last moment rang the airline and cancelled the tickets. And then sat there feeling sorry for myself.

Then, as I was still turning it all over in my mind, the 'phone rang and I got up to answer it reluctantly, feeling none-too-sociable, even when I recognised the voice as my friend George Meyer from Canberra.

'Ben!' he shouted over the long distance peeps and beeps. 'Ben, you wouldn't believe what happened today!'

'No—what, George?'

'Ben, I rode on a big shark today.' He paused to let the impact sink in.

My mind turned around wobbegongs and grey nurses, and in my irritable mood I wished George would get to the point, since I figured there must be some good reason for a long distance call.

'What kind was it, George?'

'A whale shark!' he said triumphantly, knowing it would rock me to the soles of my feet. It did.

'A whale shark?' I exclaimed, trying to form a mental picture. 'How BIG?'

'Only about twelve metres.' (My mind shrieked in silent echo ONLY about twelve metres!) George went on, obviously enjoying the surprise he had given me.

'S'truth!' I exclaimed, or perhaps something stronger.

'Yes', said George. 'I was spearfishing on that reef south of Montagu Island when this big bloke swam underneath me. The chap I was swimming with thought it was the father of all maneaters and nearly broke a leg getting back into the boat. But I knew it was a whale shark because you could see the white spots all over its back.' He paused again. 'But this is the part you won't believe. He was so quiet and steady in the water that I swam right up to him, and on impulse grabbed his tail fin. The shark didn't seem to mind, and towed me quite happily for a while. The current was pretty strong, and I could only swim up ahead of it once to look at its big mouth. I let the current drift me back, and I grabbed its dorsal fin. It must have towed me fifty metres like that. Pity you weren't there with the camera.'

A pity! That was the understatement of the year! It was a tragedy. I hadn't gone with George to Montagu that weekend because I had to prepare to leave overseas. Now I had cancelled that at the last moment, and stayed at home feeling miserable. I had missed out on one of the experiences of a diving life-time. Not to mention film—for my mind was already racing on those lines.

If I had been there with the 16 mm underwater camera the footage would have been just exactly what I needed to give lift and life to my other film on taming marine animals. What a climax it would have provided!

'Any chance he's still around, George?' I hardly dared to hope, for I knew how rare whale sharks were.

But George surprised me again. Pleasantly.

'It is possible', he said, in his strong German accent. 'The local fishermen have seen whale sharks before at this time of year, in February and March. Maybe it's the same one. At any rate they tend to hang around, and he will probably be there for a few weeks yet.'

'Terrific! It's a long shot for film but it's certainly worth a try.'

George agreed, and we discussed our plans.

I would leave for Montagu the following day, and spend the week scouting for the monster. George, who was a specialised glassblower employed at the National University, would join me on the weekend and help in the hunt. There were a lot of sharks there, as well as the usual seals, so even if we did not sight the monster the trip would not be entirely a waste of time.

Next day, filled with excitement and anticipation, I motored down to Narooma, a peaceful fishing village on the southern coast of New South Wales. Montagu Island lay 9.6 km directly seawards. Somewhere out there—hopefully—the whale shark was cruising gently on the surface, feeding peacefully on plankton and krill with no notion in his enormous sleepy head of what we had in mind for him—if we could find him—the vital 'if'.

Tuesday dawned a perfect day, with oily-calm seas and bright sunshine. A perfect setting to find the 'Big Fellow' as we now called him. With my crew I sped across an unusually calm Narooma River bar, and headed for Montagu Island—a hazy bump on the horizon, 9.7 km out in the early morning mist.

We travelled in my four-metre Caribbean Whaler boat, loaded down with gear and cameras, and the 50 h.p. Mercury did the trip in just under half an hour.

Montagu Island, though 1,609 km south of the Great Barrier Reef, is a home of big game fish and sharks. Zane Grey, the Wild West author, made the area famous on his game fishing trips before World War II and my talk the night before with Des Creighton, a local fisherman, had confirmed the habits of the whale sharks in the locality.

This one had been seen on several occasions by the fishermen, always in the area bordered by Montagu Island to the north, Aughinish Reef three kilometres south, and Pinnacle Rock 1.6 km further south-east. Apparently it cruised over these shallow reefs to scoop up plankton, and milling small trevally, which chop the surface in great schools at that time of the year.

There were other large marine animals there which also joined in on the

trevally feast; manta rays—normally found further north in tropical waters—tuna, kingfish, and smaller sharks.

In our boat we sped along the protected inside of the island, scattering the chopping schools of trevally, and Vic Ley peered anxiously down from the bow, looking for the unmistakable giant brown shape of the shark.

We sped on to Aughinish Reef, three kilometres south, where George had met the shark, and then scouted wide to Pinnacle Rock, and back along the front of Montagu Island.

Not a large shape was sighted, and except for the run-of-the-mill fish, there were only two hammerhead sharks with dorsal and caudal fins slicing the surface. Most sharks scavenge for food deeper down, but the hammerhead prefers to chase the trevally on the surface.

By the end of the week, we had covered hundreds of kilometres without a sight. We were reluctantly deciding that the whale shark had moved to other waters. Meanwhile, in Canberra, George was blowing glass, and gloomily imagining that we were riding his whale shark. He brightened visibly when he learned of our lack of success.

'You haven't seen the Big Fellow yet, boy? Don't worry, boy, we'll find him tomorrow.'

George's optimism rubbed off on us, and I waited eagerly for the next day.

On Saturday morning we were up early, with George claiming he hadn't slept a wink. 'I just couldn't stop thinking of that whale shark out there.' I knew the feeling. But overnight the weather had turned for the worse, and a huge surf on the bar greeted us as we motored up the estuary entrance.

I groaned as I saw that the pilot station had signalled that the bar entrance was closed to navigation, due to the dangerous conditions. Outside, the wind had dropped, the sea appeared moderate, and the sky was clear; yet monstrous waves crashed across the bar.

George's face was a foot long. I was dejected too. All our built-up enthusiasm was being dashed to pieces on that river bar.

'Let's at least give it a try, Ben', challenged a still optimistic George, 'we've got nothing to lose.'

Nothing to lose! Only my boat, motor, and expensive camera equipment. All my professional tools of trade which would take weeks or months to replace.

The Cropps gearing up for film work.

Eva Cropp riding a Queensland whale shark.

Looking into the mouth of a smaller whale shark off Queensland's Gold Coast.

I must have looked pretty sour at that moment. I started imagining the whale shark lolling out there on the surface, with a cynical grin on its big mouth at the plight of its unfortunate pursuers.

Yes. We had to give it a try. Dangerous bar or not.

George and I waited at the river entrance for the first lull in the pounding surf. I slowly idled the boat as far into the surf as possible, trying to gain some ground, but repeatedly swinging back when waves banked up in front of us and threatened to spill us into the surging water.

Three big waves, then a smaller one. That was the pattern, with the cycle continually repeating itself. But even the smaller ones were still three metres high. Then the surf flattened slightly as the third big wave swept through, and George standing in the bow yelled, 'Now!'

I hit the throttle, crossed my fingers, and the four-metre boat leapt ahead.

It was only a ninety-metre dash, and at thirty-seven km/h we sped diagonally between the swells to get greater speed. The boat lurched over the tops of several unbroken swells, then a giant one loomed up ahead. It was banking sharply, perhaps five metres high now, and within seconds would cap and crash down with disastrous results. I kept on the diagonal course, in the hope of beating the wave further along where it was not yet so steep. We could not go back and it was too late to chicken out. We were committed. I held my breath as the boat reared up into the big swell, poised momentarily on the peak as if undecided which way to go, then dipped down on to the seaward side.

'Phew!' I wiped my brow. 'That was a close one!'

There was surprisingly little swell beyond the breaker line, and we sped over the ten kilometres to Montagu with the refreshing thought of a pleasant day ahead.

We decided to follow the old search pattern of the triangular sweep from Montagu to the southern reefs, as surely it must give results eventually.

George stood in the bow, eyes glued downwards, and his comments on the numerous disturbances were: 'Only a school of kingfish' or: 'A small hammer-head shark'.

Just the same the schooling fish and all the activity looked promising as we turned back for another run along the island closer inshore.

We were speeding through a school of chopping trevally when George suddenly yelled, 'Look out!'

I swerved just in time to avoid a giant, brown shape under the surface. Cutting the motor, I yelled to George to drop the anchor, and slid overboard with my camera and snorkel. I did not even spend time trying to get on the SCUBA equipment. Of course we knew what it was—a shadow of that bulk could mean only one thing. The whale shark.

I swam back to where the shape had dived to avoid the boat, with excitement and apprehension mounting and wondering just what I was going to experience. Then into my vision swam the most gigantic shark I had ever seen. It was unbelievably large, some ten metres long—and the monster was lumbering towards me.

I dived to meet him, camera running, and I was awestruck by the great head, and the mouth which was nearly two metres across.

The great shape lumbered past me, not three metres away, and it seemed to take an age for the tail to finally sweep close past my head, as I panned the camera down its full length. Behind him followed an entourage of circling kingfish, large tuna, and a small whaler shark. They scattered from me.

I turned to catch up to the whale shark, and now George was beside me, swimming hard to position himself above the shark's head.

George dived, and I filmed him sweeping along the full length of the shark, and finally grabbing the tail. The shark's reaction was the only unfriendly one it was to make, as it swept George off with one sweep of that gigantic tail. But it was inquisitive, and slowly turned to see what annoying little creature had been hanging on its tail.

It swam towards us, and I dived to meet the monster head on for my first opportunity to film the great mouth. I now saw that what at first appeared to be dark growths under the jaw were a colony of sucker fish, clinging to the rough hide, and awaiting any scraps of food that might escape its huge mouth.

The shark was now barely two metres away, its mouth appearing alarmingly large in my camera viewfinder.

For the first time apprehension mounted within me. I thought: 'Shall I keep filming, or run for it?' I decided: 'If it doesn't turn in the next couple of feet, I'm getting out of its way. That mouth can suck objects in from six feet away, and I could go down sideways!'

I was just easing my finger off the camera trigger, and edging sideways to get clear, when the monster made his own decision. His head swept sideways, the colony of sucker fish scattering, and the ponderous bulk brushed past me not a metre away.

I panned the camera down its body to George, who now hung on to its dorsal fin, seemingly steering it out of my way.

Shark and rider swept into the blue haze, and since I was now out of film, I swam ecstatically back to the boat to reload. We had agreed that George would stay with the shark and await my return with fresh film.

Whale sharks, *Rhincondon typus*, grow to as much as eighteen metres in length. An eleven-metre specimen weighed twelve tonnes and our ten-metre Big Fellow we figured would be easily ten tonnes. An enormous beast.

Though growing to such a tremendous size, the whale shark is harmless. It feeds only on plankton and small fish.

Large objects do sometimes go down their throats. One whale shark, cut open in Ceylon, had a collection of boots, buttons, and uniforms in its stomach. Ditched laundry or ditched airmen? We will never know, though the question sometimes crossed my mind when I was close to the mouth doing head shots.

But it is a rare shark, and mainly inhabits the tropical seas of the world. Hans Haas photographed one once underwater, fifteen years before in the Red Sea. The Kon Tiki Expedition sighted one on their Pacific crossing, and other sightings have come from the east coast of Africa, southern California, and more recently along the Queensland and New South Wales coastline.

The whale shark's colour is usually a greenish-brown on the back and sides, marked with unmistakable white or yellow spots and narrow white or yellow transverse stripes. The underside is white, and along the full length of the body run several projecting lateral ridges.

The skin is coarse, like rough armour-plating, and this allows a sufficient hand hold to the diver. The entire prehistoric-looking body appears to be rigid, with only the latter half of the tail moving in a slow, rhythmic sweep as it lumbers on through the ocean.

Inside the mouth are masses of spongy tissue, forming a sieve-like strainer, to catch the plankton and transport them to the stomach.

I could not see any noticeable teeth, though I believe they are minute, and in thousands along the jaws. To find out would have involved getting too embarrassingly close.

With my camera now reloaded, I rejoined George ninety metres away, still following the whale shark. George said he had lost it on two occasions. But each time the whale shark returned of its own accord. As I dived to film again below its head, my bubbles rose up and tickled the clinging colony of remora fish underneath its jaw. They scattered and took up positions further along the side of the head, one actually disappearing into a long gill slit.

I filmed George as he dived again and patted the huge head. George then settled back in a sitting position with legs straddling the shark.

I was exhausted now from dragging the camera, and continually trying to keep up with the monster. As I panned the camera along its body, the two-metre high tail passed me and I grabbed on for a moment's rest and was towed too.

I swept on, with George still astride, for an exhilarating ride on our friendly transport.

Soon the film ran out again. Exhausted we fell behind the shark, which now seemed to be losing interest in our hitch-hiking.

The anchored boat was a kilometre back against the current, and with my heavy camera I could make no headway. So I swam diagonally for Montagu Island, while George struggled slowly to the boat and brought it over. But I didn't mind the long, tiring swim to shore, or the wait while George searched for me in the boat. I knew what kind of film I had in the camera and how worthwhile it had all been.

Giant waves were still crashing over the river bar when we got back. As a precaution I slipped my flippers and mask on, and sat with the valuable film safely enclosed in the waterproof camera housing which I held tightly in my free hand, prepared for the worst. But my four-metre whaler boat proved to be a good surf boat, and we rode a five-metre swell all the way to the beach. On looking back with relief over the boiling surf, I wondered whether our success was due to luck or patience—or both.

The photos, blown up from the 16-mm colour movie film, made front pages in newspapers around the world, and appeared in the top magazines, including *National Geographic*, and were the cover and major illustrations in my next book, *Whale of a Shark*.

The film, on taming marine animals, with the whale shark now included as the climax, was also titled *Whale of a Shark*. It was screened on world-wide television, including the BBC and American ABC colour network.

George Meyer riding on the back of the giant whale shark off Montagu Island in February 1965.

An American viewer, used to Hollywood-made monsters, said to me, 'I can't believe it. You must have faked that big shark. Probably a Hollywood prop.'

His 'Hollywood prop' would have cost several hundred thousand dollars. Mine cost me a week of patience, anxiety, frustration, and hard work—with a little luck thrown in.

Since then I have seen quite a number of whale sharks, and filmed and photographed them from all angles working from my new home base on Queensland's Gold Coast. The Queensland surf club air-sea rescue patrols usually give me a friendly ring when the big sharks laze their way up the coast in January and February, and it has become something of an annual event to swim with them between Great Barrier Reef filming trips.

For me the whale shark and the taming of marine creatures that year meant a complete change of direction. From that point on my films have centred entirely on living creatures. Killing has no part in any of my programmes and, like most divers who have spent long enough in the sea, I have become a convinced conservationist.

So that the whale shark, the gentle giant, was a turning point. Something to look back on and remember.

75

The Great Shark of Jurien Bay

HUGH EDWARDS

A team of two, and a good team, they were the Western Australian State pairs spearfishing champions in 1967.

Bob was twenty-four, short but strongly built and with a pleasant manner which won friends easily. He was dedicated to diving and was the secretary of the Western Australian Council of Underwater Activities and an organiser of the Australian Spearfishing Championships held at Busselton, Western Australia, in December 1967.

Lee was twenty-six. An ex-schoolteacher who made a living from diving for crayfish and from spearing fish. He had a tremendously powerful physique, very blue eyes, and a black bushy beard. He was the more brilliant diver of the two, but Bob had the best endurance and concentration. As a combination of strengths they were highly effective at their sport.

In August 1967, Bob Bartle and his bearded diving partner Lee Warner travelled the red dusty road to Jurien Bay 240 km north of Perth in a Volkswagen with their spearguns.

They were going to compete in a spearfishing meeting. As competitions went, it was a minor one. But they regarded it as important. It was practice for them for the Australian Spearfishing Championships in four months' time.

In 1967, having learned hard lessons in gear and techniques in previous championships, Warner and Bartle had the national pairs title as their goal. On their home territory they knew they had a good chance of winning against divers from the Eastern States—provided they had a solid grounding of months of hard diving practice to build stamina and sharpen techniques.

So—though the cold and sullen winter waters of Jurien Bay were hardly inviting—they were looking forward to the meeting as a test of the progress they were making. Saturday, August 19, was listed as a practice day—a chance for visiting divers to look over the ground and adapt their gear to local conditions. The actual competition, the fish-spearing, would be held the next day, on Sunday the 20th.

On the practice day Bob swung his Volkswagen off the track and braked to a halt on the high grey bluff of North Head at Jurien Bay, overlooking the area where the competition would be held.

He and Warner looked out over the reefs and breaking bomboras of the bay with practised eyes. The best ground looked to be a reef a mile or so off-shore, and, with a few wry jokes about the weather, they got their gear out and began shrugging into their rubber wetsuits. Other divers from other cars were similarly getting into their gear, and they dressed quickly from long familiarity with their suits and equipment.

Lee had on a full-length black neoprene rubber wetsuit to his ankles, while Bob's short suit only went to his knees. Both men wore close-fitting helmet hoods, and they carried the standard floats with diver's flags (red, with a white diagonal stripe) which they towed for identification and from which they would hang their speared fish from a wire toggle.

They walked down the bluff's steep slope to the water's edge, carrying their masks, and flippers, lead-belts, and big single-rubber spearguns, and after a quick look around, walked into the water, rinsed their masks and—with a grimace at the weather—began swimming.

They swam out from the grey limestone headland, heading for the deeper water about a mile off-shore, looking for big fish like kingfish, groper, jewfish, as well as the smaller fish which counted for points in competition. They swam with the hard-kicking style of professionals, working hard to get warm and cover ground.

They had no thought of sharks, though both had seen plenty on the off-shore reefs. Warner had kept himself in pocket money as a youth by shooting grey nurse and whalers for fish shops, and had had a brush or two with bigger sharks.

Bob had also been involved in shark incidents, like most of the deep reef spearfishermen, and had fought off a bronze whaler at Dunsborough in the south, jabbing it away with his loaded gun as it charged repeatedly.

After Dunsborough he had claimed, 'If anyone asks me if I'm scared of sharks I won't shrug my shoulders.'

But sharks were regarded as summer fish, active when the sea water was warm. At Jurien that August as they swam for the far-out reefs they had thought it would be too cold, much too cold, for sharks.

The bottom was weedy and featureless until about 700 m off the headland they came across a hole or depression in eight metres of water. It was about twelve metres across with overhanging ledges—the sort of place for jewfish.

'Might as well have a look', Bob said.

Lee Warner nodded agreement. 'Right-o', and Bob went down in a shallow glide, speargun in front of him and dropping the lead sinker of his float line so it would not tangle as he swam through the caves under the ledges.

There were no jewfish. They prepared to move on, and Bob dived again for his float lead. He reached the bottom, picked it up, and as he was beginning to rise, Warner turned and began to swim on.

Suddenly an enormous black shape hurtled below Warner's flippers. It was a shark so big and moving so quickly that Warner—who had seen many sharks but nothing like this—gasped involuntarily.

Without slackening speed the shark hit Bartle, seizing him between shoulder and thigh, and striking with an impact which knocked his mask off. It began to shake him violently from side to side.

For an instant Warner remained frozen by the swiftness and unexpectedness of the attack. Instinct was to flee, but Lee was not lacking in courage.

He had killed sharks before, though nothing of this size. But he knew that a spear in the tiny brain could immobilise even a giant.

Warner dived down towards the struggling shapes on the bottom, aiming his speargun as he dived.

'I went straight down and put a spear in the top of the shark's head right where I figured the brain should be. It hit with a solid clunk. But it didn't seem to affect it, except that it attracted the brute's attention to me. It sort of shook its head, then bit Bob in half and rose up at me . . .'

The shark swam upwards through a cloud of blood, the lower part of Bob still in its jaws, flippers protruding.

'Christ!' said Warner to himself, eyes bulging in horror behind his mask.

As it came at him he pushed himself away from it with the unloaded gun, jabbing at the great black eye with the butt. The eye rolled white. 'I didn't think sharks could do that.' His mind was curiously detached for a moment. But he was soon brought back to reality.

'Never in my life have I seen anything so chilling than watching that shark circling around me with the body of Bob still in its huge jaws. From less than one metre I could see the terrible wounds inflicted. I was helpless. I could see Bob was dead. That was only too obvious. I thought I was soon to follow. I simply cannot describe the terror which flowed through me. . . .'

The water was now dark with blood and shapes were distorted and indistinct—grotesque in the twilight of darkened water. The enormous shadow moved through it all.

'It kept circling about eight feet from me. Its body looked about five feet thick from top to bottom. I didn't really get a good idea of its length—I couldn't see the extremities and don't remember seeing the tail. All I could see was the eye and what it had in its mouth.'

He had a moment of mesmerised indecision.

'Then out of the corner of my eye I saw Bob's gun which was still loaded and floating just below the surface. I grabbed it gratefully, and swinging it around tried to belt the spear into the shark's eye. But the eye was set close to the top of its head and somehow the spear just whistled harmlessly over the top of its head. It was the worst shot of my life. I don't know how I could have missed, and I've cursed myself for it a thousand times since.

'That was my last real chance to get back at the shark.

'It kept swimming round and round and started getting caught and tangled up in all the lines. It was tied to my gun by the line from the first spear and my gun picked up the float lines. There was just one big tangle—a mess. I was scared of getting caught up in the lines myself.

'The shark was black on top and white on its guts. A sort of mottled pattern. It looked weird in the bad winter light and the blood-reddened water. I could see its jaw was much wider than the body—the jaw must have been a metre wide at least. Maybe more.

'I knew Bob was dead. And there was the thought of other sharks.

'A little bronze whaler came and began darting around in the blood. Were there any more big ones? I swam backwards, fast. From 100 yards away I looked back and saw the shark still moving around tangled in the lines and floats on the same spot.

'I felt pretty bloody helpless, I can tell you. But once I lost sight of it I began free-styling for shore. It wasn't too far but it seemed miles. Now and again I looked back to convince myself the shark was still back there. I was still frightened.

'I swam away from a friend and diving companion of seven years, and that's something I'll never forget. Not as long as I live.'

Warner reached the shallows and ran from the water stumbling. When he looked back he could see one or two flags and floats of other divers far out at sea, unaware of the tragedy that had taken place so close to them. It all seemed unreal—in fact the sense of nightmarish unreality never left him.

He searched for the keys to Bob's Volkswagen parked up on top of the bluff at North Head, and couldn't find them. But he found a key to one of the other cars and drove, skidding around the corners, ten kilometres along the dirt track to Sandy Cape, a crayfishing settlement, to gasp out his story and ask for a boat to get the other divers out of the water.

The season was over, but one or two boats still swung on the moorings with silent engines. Harry Holmes' *Gay Jan* was one—a thirteen and a half-metre steel boat. Harry agreed at once to go to North Head and in a short time they were off the grey headland, with the cray boat rolling in the winter swell.

They could see the two divers' floats and the tangle of lines, and something dark below them. The shark was still there.

There was something else floating too. A human torso cut through across the breastbone by the teeth of the giant shark.

Bob still had air in his lungs. Death must have been very quick, for he had not even cried out. It may be that he was never aware of what had happened, and his diving friends have always hoped so.

When they took hold of the tangled lines in the hope they might catch the beast, the shark—that vast, indistinct shape on the bottom—began to swim slowly away. It was incredibly strong. The cords snapped one by one. The metal fittings on the spears straightened out. Then it was gone.

The divers went back to Jurien Bay and held a wake that night. Next day they held their spearfishing competition as it had been planned. It was not bravado, and it was something other than plain courage.

'Bob would have wanted it that way', they said.

A massive hunt was launched for the shark and rewards were offered for its capture. But it was never seen again.

No one was quite sure even what kind of shark it was. It is a measure of the horror of that day that Warner—normally a meticulous observer of marine life—was unable to remember clearly anything about it except the great dark eye and what it had in its mouth.

The argument has never been resolved about whether it was a huge tiger, black-backed with age, or that known killer and maimer of divers, the great white shark.

The presence of breeding seals on nearby islands might explain the attack. The shark—like the one which attacked Henri Bource in Victoria three years earlier—may have mistaken Bob Bartle for a seal. But why did it pass under Lee Warner's flippers to attack the man on the sea-bed . . . ? That is a question which still occasionally faces Warner in his nightmares.

At Jurien Bay today there stands a simple memorial to Bob Bartle.

Putting the Pieces Together

JEREMY GREEN

He is a marine scientist who applies a practical outlook to his work.

The discovery of ancient wrecks in the 1950s and 1960s by sport divers all around the world from the Mediterranean to the West Indies led to trouble and conflicts between the authorities and the divers. Western Australia was no exception.

The wrecks which dated back to 1622 in Western Australia were nationalised by the State in 1964. Rewards were promised for future finds but the fact that no rewards were paid to the discoverers of the immensely valuable wrecks already located caused bitterness.

At the time of Green's arrival there had been no serious archaeological effort, no major excavation or even photographic reconnaissance, and the wrecks were being stripped by looters and souvenir hunters.

Green brought a new approach. He persuaded people of the importance of the Western Australian wrecks, and built up a strong museum team for diving work. In his first season he accomplished more than his predecessors had managed in the previous seven years, and he has exceeded this result in each of two seasons since, with the result that Western Australia now has a collection of wreck artefacts of world importance.

Green was twenty-nine when he came to Western Australia in 1971 after three years at Hull University and six years at Oxford. He began marine archaeological work in the Mediterranean at Malta in 1965, and subsequently worked in Turkey with the renowned George Bass, in Cyprus, and on Irish Armada and British ships, as well as the 1748 Dutch *Amsterdam* off Hastings.

When Jeremy Green came to Australia in 1971 he knew nothing about the use of an underwater chainsaw.

'But when you're confronted with the problem of grown oak stern timbers like the ones on the 1629 *Batavia* wreck, some of them a metre thick and as hard as the day they came out of the shipyard', he says ruefully, looking at work-scarred hands, 'you learn very quickly. A ton of learned theory won't shift your timber. You need the chainsaw, and you have to be able to survive using the thing as well as chopping the wood.'

The chainsaw is typical of the Green approach. It has its hazards—a poor operator swirled about by surge and current may take unscheduled nicks and gouges out of a three century-old wreck. Or he may even do himself some

Jeremy Green.
(*Pat Baker*)

Raising the timbers presented all kinds of problems. Here a section small enough to raise is cut with a chainsaw. Despite 334 years, the oak was hard and heavy, still had cow hair packing, and the marks of carpenters' adzes and chisels. ◄
(*Pat Baker*)

Diver working air lift on the *Batavia* wreck to expose ship's timbers. ▼
(*Pat Baker*)

damage if he becomes disoriented in the turbulence and poor visibility and loses track of the shimmering blade.

But used with skill it is a neat and time-saving method of excavating timber —part of the practical approach of the modern marine archaeologist.

Underwater archaeology is one of the youngest of the cultural sciences, made possible only by the development of cheap self-contained breathing apparatus.

Though its aims—the recovery of objects and information—are the same as land archaeology, the practice is vastly different because of the diving and because of the nature of the sea itself. As a science it has had to begin from basic beginnings. Few land archaeologists have converted to marine archaeology. Though it is comparatively easy to learn to dive to a stage where you can swim on a site, there is far more to marine archaeology than blowing educated bubbles over a dead ship.

A marine archaeologist must not only be able to dive. He must be a good diver with the stamina to spend long hours daily in the water. And he either has to gather a practical knowledge of boats and general seamanship, the use of underwater cameras, heavy lifting gear, cutting tools, and explosives, or he has to hire someone very expensive to do it for him.

Men who have succeeded—such as George Bass and Peter Throckmorton, in the Mediterranean, Robert Marx at Port Royal, Jeremy Green in Australia— have all had to contend with limited budgets and have achieved their results mainly because they are practical men able to dive and sort out the on-site problems for themselves.

One of the problems is protecting delicate or friable material such as pottery and leather, cloth, or rope (sometimes astonishingly well preserved in the remains of a centuries-old ship) while doing hard bullocking work on tough subjects such as timber, ballast, or cannon. Particularly, as often happens, when the precious smaller objects are held in conglomerate material jammed under cannon and timber. But both cannon and adjacent crockery can be raised, with skill and care.

One of the differences between treasure hunters and souvenir pickers (usually looking only for coin) and archaeologists is that to the scientist *everything* is important. They sometimes weep when they find a wreck blown apart with explosives for pieces-of-eight or dragged with nets and grapples for the 2000-year-old Mediterranean amphorae vases. Ignorance and greed all too often leave a trail of wreckage in their wake. It is the everyday things which most interest the marine archaeologist.

'A ship on a voyage is a self-contained world of her own', Jeremy Green explains. 'Apart from her equipment and running gear there are the guns and weapons for protection, victuals and cooking utensils, tools for maintenance and repair, and all the personal possessions of the people aboard—not to mention the widely-varied cargoes.

'The guns, the tools, the pots and pans, jugs, mugs, rosary beads, coins, medallions, buckles and boots were the same as those in use ashore at the time. If we know the date the ship sank she becomes a time capsule precisely dating everything inside her. This is often very difficult to do on land sites and is one of the most important aspects of artefacts recovered from wrecks.

'Also because precious metals, such as gold and silver, and also brass, lead, and pewter, tend to be melted down every so often ashore and re-used, sometimes the only surviving examples of particular types of ancient guns, navigation instruments, and coins, can be found in wrecks.'

When Jeremy first came to Australia, after diving on wrecks as old as the tenth century B.C., he had private reservations about the interest of working on 'modern' wrecks a mere 300 years or so old. But though many of the purists of Mediterranean archaeology regard anything after Roman times as so modern as to be almost suburban, Jeremy Green has found a major challenge in the Dutch-Australian wrecks.

'The Dutch were meticulous at recording detail', he says, 'and the stories of the ships we are working on are remarkably complete. This adds a great deal of life and interest to what we're doing.

'For instance our base for operations on the *Batavia* wreck is Beacon Island where the mutiny and massacres took place in 1629.

'It adds something when you read the details of the torturing and confessions of the mutineers, and the passing of their death sentences, to know that it all took place not many yards from the hut where you're reading . . .

'On the wreck we have recovered silver bowls, engraved jugs and beakers, with Oriental scenes unmistakably done by a Dutch artist. We even found a set of silver bed-posts perhaps intended for the harem room of the Great Mogul.'

An important aspect of wreck relics is that they can often be precisely dated.

The stein in perfect condition.
(*Pat Baker*)

Brass tap. ▶
(*Pat Baker*)

Tinder box.
(*Pat Baker*)

If we know a ship like the *Batavia* sank in the year 1629, we know that the things such as the silver dishes aboard her were definitely in use in that year and were made before that time.

This is interesting in terms of navigation instruments such as the astrolabes used for sun and star sighting. They were supposed to be antiquated and out of use by the end of the 1500s, but the *Batavia* in 1629 had two aboard. There was an artillery expert's entry that the little breech-loading bronze cannon known as swivel-guns were only in use, 'for a very short period because of their unreliability', but they have turned up in Columbus-era wrecks of the 1490s; in 1588 Armada ships off Ireland; and in the Dutch *Zeewyk* wreck off the Western Australian coast dated 1727. A long and useful design life-span after all.

Jeremy Green's first excavation in Australia was the 1656 *Vergulde Draeck* or Gilt Dragon at Cape Leschenault ninety-six kilometres north of Perth.

In the summer of 1971-72 the Western Australian Museum team recovered a wide variety of artefacts, including stoneware greybeard or Bellarmine jugs, brass kitchenware, 6000 pieces-of-eight, and an entire box of clay papes. Among the pipes was one depicting Sir Walter Raleigh (who first brought the tobacco of the American Indians to Europe) being swallowed by a crocodile. The legend was that the reptile disliked his nicotine pipe-tobacco taste and spat him out.

The spread of the smoking habit in Europe is well-illustrated by the wrecks. On the *Batavia* of 1629 only a very few clay pipes of a crude variety were found. The *Draeck* had one large box. By 1712 when the *Zuytdorp* went ashore clay pipes were one of the commonest items in the ship. In the sailors' camp of the *Zeewyk* in 1727, there are so many pipes that it is easy to make a collection of more than a dozen brands, for by that date the pipes were smooth and sophisticated and carried trademarks.

Running a *Batavia* culverin along the jetty at Beacon Island; Guy Wilkinson and Myra Stanbury of Western Australia Museum.
(*Pat Baker*)

84

Gilt Dragon bottle patiently assembled from fragments.
(*Pat Baker*)

Batavia napkin ring. ◄
(*Pat Baker*)

The *Batavia* excavation began in 1973 and was continued through a second season in 1974 with more work scheduled for succeeding years.

Though at first the *Batavia* appeared to be merely a sand and coral gully with a few encrusted cannon and anchors—giving the impression everything worthwhile was washed away—she has turned out to be an archaeological goldmine. The wreck and its relics were actually buried below a crust of coral. The reef had grown over the ship.

'Not everything has gone according to plan', Green points out. 'For instance, we hoped very much to find some timber, and we reasoned logically that if any had survived it would be under a great pile of stone blocks in the middle of the ship. It seemed sensible that the weight of the stone would have buried the timber or kept it out of the reach of teredo worms.

'So we moved the blocks. They weighed twenty-seven tonnes total and lifting them occupied many a long day. When we'd got them all up we found that they were cut and decorated and formed part of a portico or building facade the ship was carrying to the East Indies. This was very interesting. Nonetheless we were disappointed to find no sign of any timber.

' "Ah, well!" we thought, "it would have been nice . . ."

'Then quite suddenly we found the timber. Far more than we had ever expected—in fact about a third of the port side, more than thirteen metres long and six metres wide—in a sand hole where we hadn't thought anything would survive. That's a marine archaeologist's *Catch* 22. You have to expect the unexpected.

'Then there was the ship's bell. People always talk about bells and treasure chests, but they're not the sort of things found ordinarily. Fairy story stuff. But on almost the last day of excavation in 1973 we were working on the timbers when I noticed something green in a gully to one side. And there it was. Beautiful as any sight you could wish to see on a wrecksite. The ship's bell . . .'

In 1973, the work consisted mainly of raising the building blocks and a number of cannon, and uncovering the remains of the ship by means of air-lifts. The crew were Graeme Henderson, assistant curator, Pat Baker, the expedition's official photographer who had worked with Green in Cyprus, Guy Wilkinson, another Cyprus veteran, and the Museum's own divers Jim Stewart, Warren Robinson, Colin Powell and Geoff Kimpton. Recording work ashore was done by Myra Stanbury.

The air-lifts, long, flexible, plastic pipes like giant vacuum cleaners, worked on suction caused by passing compressed air through them and gobbled up sand and coral with a voracious appetite. They were named 'Biter' and 'Snatcher' by the crew from their disconcerting habit of inhaling divers' hands in their ten centimetre muzzles along with rocks and sediment, causing many skinned knuckles and a great deal of profanity.

1973 saw a great deal of pottery uncovered, and when Green went to Europe afterwards he was surprised to find that from the *Draeck* and *Batavia* he had one of the world's largest collections of dated Bellarmine jugs. Dates on the jugs and the various types and patterns upset several previous theories and treatises on the stoneware.

Both wrecks carried large quantities and the first assumption that they contained liquor has been revised in the face of a new theory that the Dutch may have exported mercury to the Orient in the stoneware.

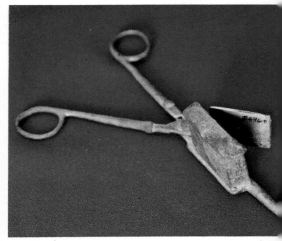

Candle snuffer.
(*Pat Baker*)

Pat Baker with a collection of the thousands of ballast bricks raised from the 1656 *Vergulde Draeck*.
(*Pat Baker*)

J. Green working on pottery identification from *Batavia* drinking stein.
(*Pat Baker*)

All artefacts and sections of the wreck had to be photographed in a regular progression, and this became doubly important when the timber was reached, for eventually each piece would be reassembled in its original position ashore after restoration.

Pat Baker photographed every rib and plank, both on the sea-bed and after it was brought ashore. Most of the timber was in an astonishing state of preservation. Hard and solid, and still showing the marks of adzes, saws and chisels of the Amsterdam shipwrights of 1627. With it came large sections of a soft pine outer layer nailed (more in hope than in real expectation of success) over pitch and cow-hair as protection against teredo worm, for it was long after the *Batavia*'s era before copper sheathing was used on timber vessels, and the East India Company was greatly troubled by worm and rot in tropic seas. But the timbers of the *Batavia*, a new ship on her maiden voyage, were untouched.

Preserving the timber—likely to dry and crack in surface conditions after three-and-a-half centuries below the waves—was a problem. Three pools were made by digging depressions in the middle of the island and lining them with plastic to soak timbers and keep them wet. Later they were wrapped in plastic with chemicals and fungicides before being sent south for complete laboratory treatment.

Meantime there were difficulties on the sea-bed.

'The first timbers were inner ribs and quite light and small', Green recollects. 'But as we dug deeper, more and more appeared and they got bigger and heavier until we were running into planks and strakes ten metres long.

'The *Batavia* timber was hard as the day it went out of the shipyard. We eventually resigned ourselves to the fact that we were going to have to saw it to cut it into workable lengths for raising and restoration.

'Our first effort was a sad joke. We took down an ordinary carpenter's saw and four hours later were exhausted after cutting only one centimetre.

'In the end we got a chainsaw and that worked fine. A good example of the kind of innovation we have to make. Archaeologically it looks terrible to see the chainsaw ripping into centuries'-old timber. But actually it makes a neat cut and the join will be indistinguishable.'

Towards the end of the five-months 1973 season the weather became rough and work had to end. The problem was the surf rolling over Morning Reef where the *Batavia* wreck lay in the breaker line. Though the divers could work sheltered in the wreck gully in quite rough conditions with waves five metres high or more thundering overhead it was impossible to keep the boat with its heavy lifting gear and deck cargo of air compressors over the wreck in safety.

In any case with ten tonnes of water-logged timber, twenty-seven tonnes of building blocks, and hundreds of lighter but historically valuable relics, the team was running into a storage and conservation problem. A break of several months would have been necessary even in ideal weather.

In 1974, work was resumed with Bob Bevaqua and Scott Sledge, of Honolulu, joining the team. Diving on the timbers brightened with the discovery of a complete gun-port and stern knees braced against a part of the transom.

'It looks as though we have the actual port side of the ship', comments Green, 'and we're hopeful of finding interesting material and perhaps even stern carvings buried underneath in 1975.'

Most of 1974 was taken up with moving a heavy concretion of cannonballs and armaments material of extraordinary variety. They included expanding bar shot, bombs, solid shot, pike, cannister, and grape shot. Enough to make a separate museum division on cannon-fired projectiles used against ships, men, and rigging.

These had all fused together in a solid mass. At first cannonballs were painfully and individually chipped out with hammer and pick. Later it was found that light fifteen-gram explosive charges detonated on top of a rubber mat broke up the concretion more cleanly and did less damage to the relics than the picks. The lesson of the chainsaw over again. Eventually more than 600 cannonballs weighing over one and a half tonnes were recovered.

There are many more seasons' work to be done on the *Batavia*, and hundreds more relics to be brought up to join the thousands already recovered.

'Each item has to be individually recorded, photographed, and drawn', says Green. 'After that they go to the conservation laboratory in our maritime museum at Fremantle.'

The conservation of the material is an enormous task. Skilled scientific treatment is needed to prevent friable materials such as wood, leather, and iron from disintegrating in surface conditions. Even durable brass and silver often need special treatment.

Dr Colin Pearson, who came to Western Australia after working on the Captain Cook cannons, is in charge of the Fremantle conservation laboratory. Some of the treatment processes last months and even years. But at the end of them the wreck objects will be stable and permanently preserved.

'This is one of the most important aspects of the work. It would be wasteful and tragic to raise things preserved three and a half centuries below the sea only to have them fall to pieces on land. One of the things which regulates our diving programme is the capacity of the laboratory to handle the material we bring up. The timber, for instance, twenty tonnes in two seasons, has given them a tremendous amount of work which they've handled extremely well.'

What will be the end result of the work on the *Gilt Dragon* and *Batavia*?

'We already have the largest collection of seventeenth century Dutch shipwreck material ever raised', Green divulges, 'and we're not finished by a long shot. There's a great deal more to do yet. After the preservation is completed we hope to reassemble the whole timber section of the *Batavia* in a shore museum together with the objects and artefacts in a way which will be really outstanding. Our work is basically putting history's pieces together so that everyone can understand their significance and see originals for themselves.'

Marine archaeology is a science which spans the centuries easily. As long as ships sail the sea and storms, misfortune, and human error send them to Davy Jones's Locker, there will be no lack of subjects for study.

Each ship is a new challenge, and a new story in human terms.

The Elingamite Treasure

WADE DOAK

In 1902 the 2,585-ton Huddart-Parker Line steamer *Elingamite* sailed from Sydney bound for Auckland, New Zealand. She had on board 136 passengers, a crew of eighty-five, and Bank of New South Wales bullion to the value of £17,320 safely locked away in the turret tank near her stern.

Four days later, rounding the northern tip of New Zealand, on a foggy Sunday morning, November 9th, 1902, sailing blind in the mist at reduced speed, she drove hard into the cliff base of steep West King Island and sank in a short time.

Many of her people were drowned in the confusion and horror of the sinking. Others were lost in a crowded lifeboat which drifted out to sea and overturned, and others died on a raft which drifted eight days before it was sighted by a search vessel which rescued the handful of survivors still clinging feebly to life.

It was not long before salvage attempts were made to reach the bullion. These added to the tragedy, costing the lives of the early helmet divers, and the wreck was abandoned.

In 1966, New Zealand divers Wade Doak and Kelvin Tarlton re-located the coin in the shattered remains of the old ship forty-six metres down under the shadow of West King.

Doak, who runs New Zealand's *Dive* magazine, and Tarlton who has a ship museum, are an enterprising and adventurous pair. They tackled the problems of the *Elingamite* in their characteristic manner.

It's no secret really if I tell you where there is a tonne and a half of pure silver lying off the New Zealand coast. At least there was a tonne and a half, until we lifted 150 kg out of the wreck.

The rest can stay there for a while. Buried under a mountain of corroding iron plates and girders in the guts of the old steamer *Elingamite*, it is just too deep and too dangerous to get at.

Already three divers have died in the attempt. And about 6,000 gold coins are down there too, still as mint and shiny as the day the ship sank. Kelly and Jag and John and I have taken twenty-one of them but that took us two years and 150 dives. We reckon the silver will do us—about $24,000 worth as metal, but some of these old Queen Victoria coins are a collector's delight, all encrusted with coral and sand, glass, coal and bits of seashell.

We sell them now in sets of three. Looking at them sometimes, all bright and shining with the sea-green encrustation cleaned off them, I find it hard to

89

The *Elingamite* in 1902 not long before she was wrecked on the Three Kings Rocks off the northern tip of New Zealand. (*Kelly Tarlton*)

Wade Doak

Discs in the sand on our last dive turned out to be coins—the *Elingamite* treasure. (*Kelly Tarlton*)

believe they spent sixty-five years on the sea-bed at the foot of the Three Kings Rocks, down with the kelp, the sea urchins, and the hapuka cod.

At forty-five metres the sea can be a pretty hostile place to men. You don't see much there that's not eating or being eaten. There isn't much colour and it's always as cold as fish blood. You don't even feel like a human down there. No weight; nothing to plant your feet square on so you can size things up. Like a patient under an anaesthetic you have a mouthpiece between your teeth and the queer, thick stuff you breathe sets your lips tingling. You feel as if you're not inside yourself.

That's how it was when I came across the *Elingamite* treasure; finning quietly from rock to rock, feeling very wet and groggy, and very aware of the forty-five metres of salt chill liquid cutting me off from the air and sky. Any sudden effort sent an icy squirt of water through the neck of my wet suit and sluiced around my armpits. Then I would get a bit dizzy and have to screw my mind into focus on what I was doing.

I'd passed Jag Gallagher and John Pettit struggling in the current to attach a shotline to a couple of portholes, and Kelly was drifting around with his huge camera rig and flash gun.

I was starting to get clumsy from nitrogen narcosis. The thick, compressed air which I gulped from my regulator was cold too and I felt flayed and water-sodden, mind wandering a little as I nosed about the wreckage.

'Why does a man like diving?' I was thinking, 'when it can become just a matter of miserable endurance of danger and discomfort near the end of a deep dive . . .'

At that moment I found the coins.

Coins! A mound of scattered discs in the white sand. 'Is this really ME?' There was a sense of complete unreality, and detachment—like watching a film. But the coins were real enough. I shoved a handful in my plastic bag, in reflex action, like pinching myself to see if I was awake.

Gold?

I plunged my hand back into the sand feverishly. 'Too light—just pennies. May as well keep digging. Could be something better below.'

Varying-sized coins began to tumble into view. These could not all be pennies but they were not heavy enough for gold. Everywhere in the rocky recess coins were scattered, coral encrusted or sulphated black.

Then I began to worry again. 'How the hell will I find this spot again when I go up?' I should have brought down a marker buoy to fix to the kelp growing on top of the rock. 'Never mind. Grab as many as you can while you're here . . .'

This was the last dive of the expedition. I knew my air was getting very low and I shepherded every breath. The decompression meter on my wrist indicated that ascent should be made soon if I was to avoid a 'bend'.

A tap on my leg. I turned and there was Kelly wanting to know what I was doing. I flashed some coins at him. Gasping the remaining air from his tank he snapped some photos of me with his electronic flash, and ascended.

My own tank was giving me the last air we would be able to breathe on the *Elingamite* site.

'Pit-a-pit-a-pit', my sonic air pressure gauge triggered off its staccato warning forcing me to accept that it was all over as I made a last fossick through the sand, squeezed the water out of my coin bag and backed out from the underhang.

A blue wall of current was sweeping down over the wreck. I kicked off into it but I could not rise far from the bottom with the weight of coins. Removing my mouthpiece, my chilled lips fluttered uselessly around the tube of my buoyancy compensator as I puffed in some air; like a yellow halter around my neck it swayed and tilted, inflated by my exhaust. I lightened and lifted off. The current started to bear me away. Slanting up from the wreck I tried to fix some landmarks in my mind as I rose faster and faster towards the surface and our vessel the *Ahiki* somewhere up there.

My mask burst through the surface. 'Wait till the boys see this bullion!' I thought, clutching on to the precious bag. The surface was a mad, white confusion in the tide race. The *Ahiki* was soaring or plummeting with the deep swells as she cruised as close in as she dared.

Despite the evening sunlight my yellow buoyancy compensator was quickly seen. Sea birds swooped low over me. Bucking violently the *Ahiki* swung her bow around and came surfing down. One moment her red bottom was indecorously exposed, the next I was looking down on her foredeck winches and gear. Alternately I soared high on a crest or dropped under her hull. She could not use her propeller in case it hacked into me, and I had to back off smartly to avoid her crashing bilge. 'How could Kelly make it with his great, unwieldy camera rig?' flashed through my mind.

Both the ship and myself were being swept north, away from the sea-lashed

Expedition members: (L. to R.) Kelvin Tarlton, John Gallagher, Peter Clements, Wade Doak, Jeff Pearch, and John Pettit, with gold and silver on deck.
(*Kelly Tarlton*)

island. With a series of strong fin thrusts I snatched the ladder and friendly arms reached down to help me aboard.

They grabbed the bag from me to safety, and by the time I had flung my gear off the boys were crouched in a circle on the counter of the ship: John Gallagher (Jag), John Pettit, John Young, Kelly Tarlton, Jeff Pearch and Mr Tarlton, Kelly's father. On a sack in their midst was a small heap of gritty, rust-covered coin. Jag wielded a hefty diving knife and started to hack, scratch and gouge at a coin, hopeful of a golden gleam.

It was silver instead. The *Elingamite* treasure.

Later it was strange to think that the wreck hadn't really figured in our plans. We had gone to the Three Kings for spearfishing and photography. It was an area of deep spectacular underwater cliffs and drops and huge kingfish and hapuka groper. We would never have gone there but for the monster fish, because the remote rocks out of sight off New Zealand's northern tip are difficult and expensive to get to.

Though we knew the bones of the *Elingamite* were out there, and that she had taken £17,300 or $34,600 down with her, we had thought she would be too deep, and the chances of finding her too remote.

Up till then spearfishing had been our main impetus in going to the Three Kings. But after we found the coins, our spearguns were all but forgotten. After that, of course, all we could think of was the treasure.

On the return trip a fortnight later we started badly. Stuck in the mud of the Awanui River on a falling tide on our way out to sea and we had to endure two hours' vile mud stench and frustration.

But after that things went well. Our crew were myself and Kelly, John Pettit, and John Gallagher, and for once the weather was kind. We had five days of hard and entirely satisfactory diving on the wreck. John Pettit found the first gold half sovereign on his first dive, and that fired the rest of us.

During the following days, over fifty descents were made into the boiling rip that swirls around the West King. Our team accumulated over twelve hours at forty-five metres.

By starting diving early in the morning and finishing at the last evening light we were able to dive three times a day, in two shifts.

With each descent to the wreck we felt a keen edge of excitement. Silver wasn't enough—this time we might lay our hands on the gold. In the vicinity of our initial finds we discovered numerous pockets of coins. The fifty-two wooden bullion boxes must have crashed together and split in this area. As the wreckage crumbled and settled, fierce undersea currents plucked up coins and lodged them in crevices and holes; or else they remained buried under the corroding debris.

We used two airlifts like giant vacuum cleaners, to suck away the sand over-burden and expose the coins, embedded in black seams of oxidised steel plates. The exhaust from our SCUBA regulators, rattling up the alkathene pipe of the airlift, created a powerful vortex at the intake. We were always in a hurry. At depth, time is an enemy.

With picks, crowbars, screwdrivers and knives we levered out silver coins. Some came individually, others came off in great black chunks of tumbled half-crowns, florins and shillings. The immense pressure of the collapsing wreck had flattened some coins to wafer thinness, or doubled them around plates. Some coins were found adhering by their edges to the roof of a cave. At some time

they would have rested on piled wreckage which had later disintegrated leaving them welded in place by corrosion and coral growth.

As we toiled, each diver imagined that the next handful would reveal gold coins lying in a thick bed just like the silver he was tearing away. Somewhere, very close to us, under the wreckage, the gold must be heaped, still shiny, not corroded into great lumps like this silver. Perhaps beneath a bright blue sponge

or a patch of lolly-pink coral. We were finding coins everywhere in the vicinity among the litter of broken champagne bottles, twisted lead pipes, encrusted portholes, eroded girders and porcelain bathroom tiles. Each shift, some divers would mine coins, while one prospected for fresh deposits.

Without our decompression meters, buoyancy compensators and contents gauges, so many descents in such hellish conditions could hardly have failed to produce an accident. Since recompression facilities were twenty-four hours away in Auckland there could be no mistakes. Conventional diving tables involve human error. This risk would be too great when five divers would be using them for repetitive dives under difficult sea conditions.

Our five automatic decompression meters offered the safest means of calculating our repetitive diving pattern and we followed them to the letter.

A spare SCUBA set and relief divers were always ready on the *Ahiki*, patrolling as close in as possible.

I was working on a deep sand excavation on the second dive of the day, shovelling coins out and tossing them on to the rock sill to be gathered later. Through a flurry of sand and silver a gleam of gold flashed. Feverishly I snatched

Gold. ◄
(*Kelly Tarlton*)

The treasure on deck.
(*Kelly Tarlton*)

up the sixpence-sized disc. St George and the dragon shone through the light covering of reddish algae. Suddenly all consciousness of numbing cold and depth vanished. I finned over to where Kelvin was fossicking nearby. I grabbed him by the leg, waving the coin at him doing a crazy haka and gushing bubbles.

I tore back into my diggings and soon found five more gold coins. Too precious to entrust to the sack, I slipped them into my face mask where I could literally keep an eye on them as I worked.

We dived until the last light. After the final shift had surfaced in the sun-flecked tide-race we had eleven golden coins in the wheel-house: still shiny after sixty years of immersion which had reduced a steel ship to ruin, they evoked a new respect for gold. Man's idolisation of it in a changing universe seemed more understandable. Each was a tangible link with the disaster: dated 1902 they would have been in mint condition when the *Elingamite* sank.

Next morning a north-west wind was howling around the wreck site. A swing to the north-east was coming. We tried one more dive in a desperate bid to locate the rest of the gold, but plunging seas and rising winds cut this short. Our air supplies and food were virtually exhausted anyway.

On that trip, my logbook records, we raised eleven gold half-sovereigns, 1000 half-crowns, 400 florins, and 3000 shillings—thirty-six kilo weight of silver. Though it was no fortune, it whetted our appetite, naturally, for another attempt a year later.

There was a lot to do first. We had to establish who the legal owners of the coin were. We needed more efficient gear for sorting coins from rubble below and there was historical research to do into the story of the *Elingamite* herself—the most absorbing task of all.

It was remarkable how much was available. We found that one of the survivors of the 1902 wreck was still alive, with vivid memories of the steamer striking the vertical rock face of West King in the fog at 10.40 a.m. on that Sunday, 9th November, 1902. The day of King Edward's birthday in London.

He was Nahum Cassrels who was a little boy of seven or eight at the time.

'I was travelling with my mother on the way from Sydney to Auckland', he told us. 'I was playing around on the ship at the time. It was a very, very dense fog, so thick you could hardly see more than a few yards in front of you. Occasionally it would rise a bit forward of the bridge where the officers with their sextants were trying to take a shot of the sun but there was no sun for them to see.

The foghorn was going continuously. There were a number of people around, I think, mostly womenfolk. All of a sudden there was an all-out cry. The bell rang. I remember hearing the bell ringing; apparently it was a bell for the ship to go full speed astern. The fog lifted just at that moment when before us were the rocks. There wasn't any possible hope. I can't remember any severe impact but a ripping noise seemed to go through the ship. There was a tremendous scream from the womenfolk and others in which I joined. Asked later on why I screamed I said: "Well, everybody else screamed", which was quite a reasonable thing to say.

'However, the next thing was a rushing around, everyone clearing off and apparently my mother and myself were left on the foredeck. I was frightened and crying. Mother took me up to the port side of the ship. The ship had swung right round from head on, against the rocks and the two of us looked over the side. She said: "There you are, boy, it's quite all right, it's only a wharf we have come into. Don't be frightened." And if my mother said it was only a wharf we had come into, well I was quite satisfied and I wasn't frightened any more.

'I can remember also while looking over, the water dripping from beetling cliffs which were right over the top of us and coming down on to my head. We were right up close in and directly under the rocks . . .

'I was thrown into lifeboat No. 3 by Mr Chalmers. I can't remember Mother getting in, but one horrible incident I do remember. A man followed me, a shortish chap with a moustache. He took hold of the lifeboat gunwhale and as it swung out it dragged him from the side of the ship. I was standing looking right down into this man's face when he let go and fell into the sea, and I saw him sucked under the vortex of the ship as she swung back the other way. I will never forget his face. I will never forget the incident. It is written indelibly on my mind until the day I die . . .

'Going through the wreckage I remember seeing a hand come up and grab an oar. A last dying action I suppose, because they couldn't pull the person in. I remember seeing the old man dead in the water and my pet magpie saying, "Caw, Caw!" in a very weary voice before he drowned. Poor little thing . . .'

After talking to Nahum Cassrels, Kelly and I found that there were several expeditions in the years immediately after the wreck which claimed the lives of two, and possibly three, helmet divers, and injured others, until the whole thing was given away as just too damned dangerous.

Wade Doak at spot where *Elingamite*'s bow crashed into the rocks in 1902. (*Kelly Tarlton*)

The son of one of the dead divers was still alive, Mr Harper of Leigh. We went to see him and found he had on his wall a picture of the schooner *Huia* on which his father had died in 1907, on the seventh expedition.

'The gold was in the turret head above the propeller shaft', recounted Diver Harper's son. 'Ted, my brother, and I were in the longboat moored fore and aft over the wreck with four anchors tendering Dad's hose. He said the bullion must have shot out when the turret head split open . . . there were fifty-two or fifty-four boxes. . . .

'In the morning dive he pulled up $804. That was a very great deal of money in those days. He was excited and told us that there were half-sovereigns stacked on their edges sticking to the iron. He even found coin sticking in the prong of a fork . . .'

Diver Harper, a man of sixty, powerfully built, who owned a hotel in Little Omaha, had had a great deal of diving experience and was regarded as the best helmet diver in New Zealand. He had raised a sunken steamer off Colombo, and laid the twenty-five ton stone blocks for the harbour breakwater there, and done a lot of harbour work in Wellington.

But the *Elingamite* was deep. Deeper than he had ever worked before. And there was the gold. It was the death of him.

There was no understanding of the effect of pressure, the 'bends', or safe working time below in those days. He had one warning on January 6th when he complained of 'deep water pains' and fainted on the *Huia*. But he recovered, and the warning went unheeded.

On 22nd January, 1907, having already brought up $1,700 in salvaged coin, the weather was perfect (fatally calm) and Harper was anxious to make the most use of the good conditions. He made three dives, staying down forty minutes on the last occasion. It had been agreed that he should come up after fifteen minutes, but the lure of the gold was too strong.

'Dad was a fine diver', old Mr Harper told us. 'He had been down one-and-a-half hours altogether that day. He was chipping the coins out with a hammer and a marlin spike. Ted, my brother, signalled him to come up, but he wouldn't. He was too excited.'

The old man's eyes misted as he told us of the death of his father sixty years before.

Diver Harper complained of feeling ill when he reached the surface. He was taken to the *Huia* and collapsed, dying a few hours later. Death was ascribed to 'heart failure'.

In that same year, the scientist John Haldane published his diving tables in England which could have saved Harper's life. Kelly Tarlton and I calculated from the *Huia* logs that, to make a safe ascent on that last dive Harper should have decompressed for 19 minutes at nine metres, 37 minutes at six metres, and 71 minutes at three metres—a total of 127 minutes! Instead he came straight to the surface and his death.

On a later expedition in 1908 using the *Claymore*—then a new, smart little ship, later to be used at the very end of her life in 1940 on the *Niagra* gold salvage—they took a diver named Clarke to meet a similar fate. Records are vague but it is believed another diver, Percy Leigh, also died on the unlucky *Elingamite* before expeditions were finall abandoned, with only $3,700 recovered.

After tracing the owners and buying the wreck for a bargain NZ$50, on our final trip in December, 1968 with Kelly, myself, John Pettit, John Gallagher, Jeff Pearch, Peter Clements and Jaan Voot, we raised $12,000 of silver and a little gold, in our most determined assault on the *Elingamite*.

This time we used the benefits of Kelly Tarlton's harbour works experience of explosives—he was known as Master Blaster for the entire trip.

The explosives were tricky to use at that depth and in the fierce surge and tide of the Kings. But Kelly did a first-rate job, opening up the coin area in the wreck.

The very first charge—fourteen plugs of gelignite and cortex—had a spectacular result. When I surfaced my yell of excitement scared hell out of everyone—they thought I had been injured.

'It's as big as a leg of mutton', I gabbled as waiting arms yanked me aboard the *Lady Gwen*. Everyone was agog for news of the effect of the explosion. 'Fantastic bloody sight', I exulted. 'Pull up the bag—bring up that bag', I yelled, to no one in particular. Out in the dinghy two men heaved and swore as a great weight slowly inched up from twenty-two fathoms. Our movie cameras whirred and tape reels spun as on the heaving deck of the *Lady Gwen* the coin sacks were emptied. A cascade of silver poured out. We danced around for joy, picking up stray beauties and raving. These coins were in first rate condition, coming from the big mass broken open by the explosion. There was no corrosion. In this one descent we had raised over fifty-nine kilo weight of pure silver. Nearly twice as much as on the whole of the last expedition. One lump weighed nearly forty-five kilograms. No wonder I couldn't get off the bottom with it. Where the rope was attached the bag was badly ripped. We had almost lost it!

So it went on day after day for a long week until the weather drove us away. Hard diving, until even pulling up fistfuls of silver became near-monotonous.

We had 10,000 *Elingamite* coins in steel ammunition boxes. The rest of the silver, and the gold, is still at the Three Kings; under the twisted plates of the old ship—somewhere.

The
South Australian
Shark Attacks

BRIAN RODGER AND RODNEY FOX

Shark attacks around the world form puzzling and inconclusive patterns. Some places where sharks are plentiful have never known an attack. Other places similar in climate, geography, and general conditions have had more than their share of fatal encounters between man and shark.

Scientists' theories about high water temperatures triggering shark activity have also been thrown overboard by cold water attacks in Tasmania, Victoria, New Zealand, and Western Australia.

In some instances areas which have been considered entirely safe for many years with no previous shark incidents may suddenly have an isolated and horrifying series of attacks which leave them with an ill-reputation for years.

Whether attacks in series are caused by a single rogue shark or other factors is open to argument. But for four years in succession, from 1961 to 1964, a white shark struck a skindiver every year along Australia's southern shores. The fourth and final attack in the series was Henri Bource, who lost a leg off Lady Julia Percy Island in Victoria in 1964. The other three were close together in locality, involving competition spearfishermen in remarkably similar circumstances.

Aldinga Beach, with its fringing reef, lies in St Vincent's Gulf, about fifty-five miles south of Adelaide.

It is one of a series of southern curving beaches with high red bluffs on the peninsula which ends with Cape Jervis and the view of Kangaroo Island standing high across the water.

Aldinga is a pleasant beach, a favourite with families, and, up to the 1960s, regarded as entirely safe. The offshore reefs provide good ground for fishing and it used to be a favourite choice for spearfishing competitions because it pleased both the reef-swimming divers and their friends and families who spent the day on the beach.

Its notoriety began on a Sunday, March the 12th, 1961, when the Cuda Spearfishing Club, and the Underwater Sporting and Photographic Association held their annual spearfishing competition.

The president of the association, a South Australian state champion, and one of Australia's top competitive divers, was Brian Rodger. At 21 years, 2.35 metres in height, with a huge frame and impressive physique, he was at a physical peak after a summer-long diet and exercise programme.

His strength and fitness were to be vital factors in the events of the day.

South Australia's last shark attack had been in 1946, and only three other attacks had been recorded since 1836. It was thought that divers were relatively immune to shark attack. Though there had been occasional incidents when whaler sharks stole speared fish from the floats divers trailed behind them, they were regarded more as a nuisance than a danger.

Only the week before at Aldinga, Rodger had a 2.7 metre whaler—the biggest shark he had seen up to that time—make a pass at his fish as he was threading a Blue Devil on to his float. And another shark of unknown size had gobbled twenty-three kilos of fish, plus a pair of plastic shoes, off another diver's float.

Brian Rodger remembers being annoyed about that incident because the shoes had belonged to him. But at the time the size of a shark which could bolt down all that fish (and the shoes) at a bite carried no significance for him.

On March 12th, the competition was drawing to a close. By lunch-time after four and a half hours in the water Rodger already had a good bag of fish, including all the common species except a herring kale. He decided to try to add a kale to his tally and swam to a deep ledge a long distance from shore where he had seen some kale previously.

He speared two kale and a morwong there and, about a kilometre from shore, was making his way back about 2.30 p.m.

Suddenly he was surprised to see two large mulloway kingfish, twenty-five to thirty kilos in weight, flash beneath him.

'Now there's an unusual thing', he thought. In all his years of diving in South Australian waters he had not seen these kingfish in open water before. They passed too quickly for a shot. But there was always the chance they would come back, since kingfish are inquisitive creatures.

'Funny thing, those kingies', he thought to himself, 'who knows?—might even see a big shark today.'

He had never seen a really big shark, and rather looked forward to it as filling a gap in his diving experience.

The irony of it was one of those strange things remembered long afterwards. The casual thought followed by reality. But a reality of a kind he could never have imagined.

He prepared to dive after the kingfish, relaxing to take a good deep breath when suddenly his whole body was thrown into a contraction of pain and fear, and he screamed through his snorkel as something sharp and ragged and terribly heavy seized his leg and hip and shook him with tremendous force.

As the teeth tore through flesh and sinew he twisted round to find himself looking into the black demon eyes of a 3.6-metre white pointer shark which had the lower part of his body gripped in his jaws.

'I read once about jabbing a thumb into a shark's eye to make him let go, and tried to reach around with my left arm. Instead of getting his eye I jammed it down his throat, and slashed the arm to the bone on his upper teeth. . . .

' "You'll have to be good to get out of this one!" I thought.

'Surprisingly he did let go, and then came back in a fast, tight circle for another bite. That was really terrifying because now I could see the whole shark and the size and enormous power of him.

'But at least I had my gun and now I had room to use it. As he came around I slammed a spear into the top of his head, about seven centimetres behind the eye . . .

'It hit him hard, stopping his charge while he threw his head from side to side to shake out the 1.5-metre stainless steel spear. He managed this soon enough. But it was strange how even though I knew I was badly hurt myself I got a thrill from planting the spear into something so large and powerful.

'It was quite irrational, but for a moment that was all that mattered and I felt pleased and excited.

'Then his spade tail flicked away into the murk, and left on my own I realised just how serious my position was. Looking down at my leg, laid open to the bones, in enormous rents from which the blood clouded, and at my shredded and lacerated arm, I knew that unless I could stop the bleeding I wouldn't make the distant shore. The actual wounds wouldn't kill me, but the loss of blood would.

'For a moment or two I wasn't sure what to do. But I found, astonishingly enough, that I could still move my leg, and figured that if I could swim I had a chance of making shore.

'I'd done a first aid programme as a part of the State's Underwater Emergency Rescue Squad course, and the knowledge I'd picked up there was pretty useful.

'About halfway back to the beach, I realised that I was weakening from loss of blood. It occurred to me that the rubber from my speargun made a natural tourniquet, and I twisted it tight over my upper thigh with my knife, jamming the handle under the bottom of my wet-suit jacket. That stopped the blood flow a bit, and I began the longest swim of my life.

'It seemed to take forever. I kept watching the beach, and it didn't seem to be coming any closer. Gradually I was getting weaker and weaker.

'I'd ditched my gun, and lead-belt, and the float with all my fish. With reluctance. Silly how a few points for a competition and a few dollars' worth of gear seemed so important when my own life was at stake. The fish float was borrowed. It didn't allow any blood to trail as it was shaped like a closed-in three-foot row boat with a tin-inch hole on top, but I had to really force myself to abandon them.

'So I plodded along, weaker and weaker, keeping going only by determination until it became difficult to breathe even through a snorkel. I rolled on my back and kicked along that way for a while.

'The land, beautiful land, came closer. I waved and yelled, "Shark!"

'But it seemed to have no effect on the people on the beach. I was about at the end of my strength and was just despairing at the waste of vital energy when a row-boat appeared with two young spearfishermen rowing for all they were worth.

' "Hang on! We'll be right with you!"

'It was only a seven-foot boat. I'm pretty big and heavy and it was obvious we couldn't all fit in. Without hesitation one of them jumped out into the bloodied water—where the shark might have still been lurking for all they knew—and helped heave me in. He swam behind pushing to help the boat along. Pretty brave stuff, I thought.

'From then on everything was OK. A whole lot of divers ran across the reef and picked the boat up bodily to carry it to shore. There was a St John's Ambulance man there. They rigged an old door as a stretcher and hauled me up the cliff—white and blue around the face by this time from loss of blood—and the police organised an ambulance dash to Royal Adelaide Hospital.'

Rodger had lost four litres of blood from his giant frame. Only his strength and fitness saw him through. He had more than 200 stitches in a three-hour operation.

The effectiveness of the repair work by Dr Matuzek and Dr Hyde was shown when after sixteen days in hospital and two months recuperating at home he was back diving again. Later in 1961 he set a new Australian free-diving record by swimming down 45.4 metres in a Mt Gambier lake on a single breath.

A year later he ran a close second to Ron Taylor (later World Champion) in the Australian Spearfishing Championships in Western Australia, and won the Championship aggregate.

Rodger's attack severely shook the confidence of South Australian divers. But as months passed the rawness of the memory waned, and it began to be treated as a freak occurrence, unlikely to be repeated.

On Sunday, December 10th, 1962, sixteen-year-old Jeff Corner and a friend Allen Phillips were swimming in a spearfishing competition at Caracalinga Head, twenty-two kilometres south of Aldinga where Rodger had been attacked in the previous year.

Jeff was the South Australian junior champion. He and Phillips were swimming about 182 m offshore with a surf ski, in water about eight metres deep with fair visibility about 1 p.m.

Phillips had just dived near Corner looking for crayfish when he saw a disturbance in the water near his friend. At first he was pleased, thinking Corner had speared a large fish—then he saw the tail of a big shark break water.

'Probably pinching fish off the float', he thought, but as he swam over and ran into a welling cloud of blood he knew with a chill certainty what had happened.

He swam for the ski, and sick to the stomach with horror, paddled across to where Corner lay on the surface in a pool of his own blood with the shark gripping his leg.

'I grabbed Jeff and tried to pull him on to the ski. But the shark, which I recognised at once as a white pointer from its pointed snout and black eye, tugged him down and out of my grasp, under the ski.

'Jeff came up again on the other side of the ski, and I caught him by the shoulders. The shark still refused to let go, and I banged it with the paddles. Hard.

'Then for no especial reason it released its grip and just lay on the surface watching us. I tried to pull Jeff on to the ski. He just looked at me, unable to speak, and his eyes rolled back. I think he was dead then. His leg was terribly mutilated, stripped of flesh from the hip to the knee.

'The white pointer just lay there and watched, cold and calculating. I cut the fish off the float and threw them over to distract him, but he took no notice, just kept watching us. Then I found Jeff's hand spear was stuck in his good leg, and jerked it free and prodded at the shark with it. But he didn't even seem to feel it.

'I couldn't get Jeff right on to the ski, and so I paddled for all I was worth with one leg hooked round his body. The shark followed. At any moment it could have made a rush and tipped us over, or dragged us off the ski.

'Then another spearfisherman, Murray Brampton, came paddling across.

' "Keep going!" he shouted, and I saw him lift his paddle and bang it down on the shark. That gave us the break we needed.

'Soon after I reached the beach, and they said Jeff was dead.'

Corner's parents and Phillips' own wife and child were on the beach.

A year later, on another Sunday morning, December 8th, 1963, the third attack took place.

This time the scene was Aldinga again, close to the spot where Brian Rodger was hit in 1961, and the occasion was the 1963 South Australian State Spearfishing Championships. The victim was Rodney Fox, the 1962 South Australian champion, strongly favoured to retain his title in 1963.

It may have been that he had unwittingly saved Rodger's life in 1961. Fox was swimming near him when Brian was attacked and though he was unaware of Rodger's desperate situation he himself was circled by a large and aggressive white shark which came so close at times that he could have touched it with his gun. He kept diving to the bottom, edging shorewards, and the shark stayed with him ten minutes or more.

Fox thought later that it was probably the shark which had attacked Rodger, now following the diffused blood trail. The distraction offered unintentionally by Rodney Fox may have allowed Rodger to escape and possibly saved his life.

At Aldinga in 1963, because of the previous attacks, the organisers of the Competition had boats picking up competitors' catches to avoid attracting sharks.

A boat was close to Fox, whose total of fish already made him a likely winner, when they heard the scream, 'Shark! . . . Shark!' and saw him threshing in blood-stained water.

He had been gliding across the bottom, speargun extended in front of him, drifting in for what should have been a perfect head shot on a nine kilo dusky morwong. A clincher for the title. . . .

Fox was about a kilometre from shore, on the edge of a deep water drop-off from seven to eighteen metres, with less than an hour of the competition left to go. As his finger tensed on the trigger he sensed, rather than felt, everything go still in the water around him.

'It was a silence. A perceptible hush. . . . Then something huge hit me on the left side with enormous force and surged me through the water. I knew at once what had happened—and was dazed with horror.

I felt sick, nauseous. My mask was knocked off, and everything was blurred, and there was a queer sensation as though all my insides were squeezed over to one side. I reached out behind and groped behind for the shark's eyes. At that point it let go of me, and I pushed my arm down its throat by accident.

With the release of the pressure uncontrollable agony swept over me in waves. But at least I was free. As I kicked for the surface and air I felt the shark under my flippers all the way. As I gulped air I felt the scrape of his hide and wrapped myself around him so he couldn't bite again.

The shark took me back to the bottom. We rolled around scraping rocks and weed and I let go, desperate again for air.

On the surface there was red everywhere. My own blood. And through it the head of the shark appeared, conical snout, great rolling body like a rust-coloured tree trunk.

Indescribable terror flowed through my body, but just before it reached me, it veered away and I felt the tug of the fish float on my belt. The shark had grabbed my fish float and suddenly I was jerked below again, and towed nine or twelve metres or more on my own line. It seemed ridiculous to die of drowning after all I'd been through. But my fumbling fingers couldn't undo the belt to which the line was attached.

Then the line parted—perhaps on the shark's teeth—and I floated up to the surface . . .'

They dragged Rodney Fox into the boat and the men there, friends of his, were almost sick when they saw the extent of his injuries. His rib cage, lungs, and upper stomach were exposed by great flaps of skin and sinew flayed back. His arm was ripped to the bone. His lungs were punctured, ribs crushed from the enormous bite of the shark.

His friend Bruce Farley kept him bending forward huddled in the bow of the boat to keep the wounds closed.

'We knew he was bad. But we didn't open up his wetsuit to find out the full

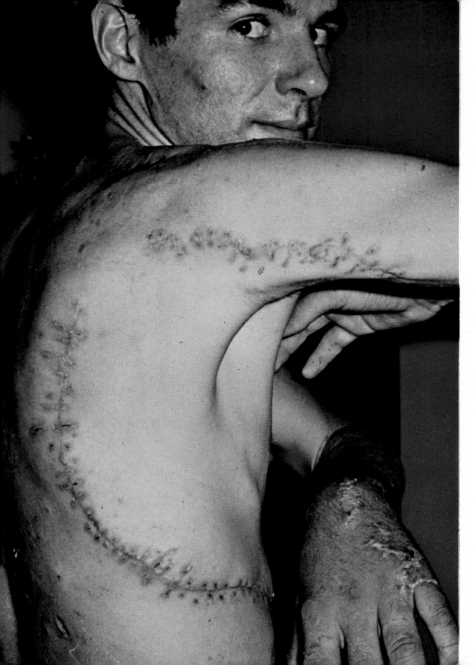

extent. We made that mistake with Brian Rodger and his leg fell apart.' Keeping the suit on was to be a vital factor.

Farley organised the beach rescue, finding a policeman almost as soon as he jumped ashore. 'He knew all the right numbers to ring.' And they got Fox into a private car and began driving him towards Adelaide while an ambulance dashed south to meet them. He was in hospital fifty-five kilometres away less than an hour after being picked up by the boat. He was lucky enough to find a surgeon on duty who had returned that day from doing a specialised course on chest operations in England.

Rasping and choking in his own blood Fox was so close to death that he heard someone at the hospital suggesting they should call a priest.

'But I'm a Protestant', he choked indignantly before the significance sank in.

Fox's toughness and physical fitness carried him through. But there is no doubt if it had not been for the speed with which he and Brian Rodger were got to the operating theatre they would have shared Jeff Corner's fate. Both were on their last reserves of strength with such severe loss of blood that another hour without expert aid and transfusion would surely have been too much even for their exceptional constitutions.

It was significant that neither of them went into shock—a factor which kills many shark victims.

Apart from their superb physical fitness this may have been because, as divers, they were familiar with sharks and had, without realising it, psychologically prepared themselves for surviving an attack.

In 1964, the South Australians won the Australian Spearfishing Championship Teams event. In the South Australian team were Brian Rodger, Bruce Farley, and Rodney Fox.

With Fox's experience the series of white shark attacks in St Vincent's Gulf ended. It may have been partly because the third attack was the last straw for many South Australian divers, who turned to safer sports and spearing competitors dwindled in numbers to a few diehards.

Or it may simply have been part of the unpredictable pattern of attacks everywhere. No one really knows why they start, or why they stop.

Except the sharks.

Swimming
with
Sea Snakes

EVA CROPP

She admits that she enjoys the fine edge of fear. 'I get a feeling high in my chest. A sort of thrill brought on by a sense of danger. It's hard to describe really.'

This temperament helps her diving work. She has hand-fed and ridden sharks in aquariums for the benefit of goggling tourists, and ridden whale sharks in the open sea with her husband Ben Cropp for her own pleasure.

Some of her most tense diving has been film work with Ben using sea snakes among the reefs off the Queensland coast and the Coral Sea. This involves handling the snakes and occasionally provoking them past the point of attack.

Though there are differences of opinion about how far a snake—like a shark—can be pushed before it will bite, there is no argument about the fact that the bite of all sea species is poisonous. In some cases several times more deadly than a land cobra or tiger snake.

While liberties can be taken with a swimming sea snake which would be fatal with a quick-striking, long-toothed tiger on land, the knowledge of the potency of the poison is disconcerting in the face of a sustained attack. Yet this kind of action is just what is required in filming the creatures. 'Ben likes a strong reaction', Eva explains.

When the reaction comes and the reptile convulses into attack she is closest to the snake.

Eva Cropp's first experiences with snakes were in a ramshackle farm-house near the Queensland border, not long after her family had come out from Hungary.

'We had an outside bath-house', she remembers, 'and I was having a shower, aged about twelve at the time, when I heard a dreadful squawking overhead.

I looked up and swinging from the rafters less than half a metre above my head was this red-bellied black snake, swaying to and fro with a screaming frog in its mouth.

I screamed so loudly myself it was a wonder the old bath-house didn't collapse around me. Then I threw the towel away—and ran! And ran!

It was a bad beginning, I guess, but in that part of New South Wales you just get used to snakes after a while. We'd get out the mix-master bowl and find a tiger snake coiled up in it. Or be running down a path downhill and find a snake coiled on the track.

You couldn't stop, so you just jumped high in the air . . . and hoped. . . . Snakes are a fact of life in the bush. So by the time I became involved in Ben's underwater filming of sea snakes I'd had a good grounding.

That's to say I had a caution of snakes. Anything that can kill you deserves respect. But I had no psychosis about them. No reptile-repulsion thing.'

I must admit the first sea snake I met gave me a bad time. It was while we were making one of Ben's films. He likes a strong reaction in his shots, and he sure got one this time.

It swam up to me quite slowly at first. I thought, "This isn't too bad. What's all the fuss about? . . ."

But then it speeded up. I kicked, which made it furious, and it attacked. The more I kicked the more it darted at me, and when I missed, it dodged past my flipper. I was all too aware of the fact that I had no protective wetsuit on.

I still have a vision of its head with beady eyes and forked tongue flickering in front of my mask. After that I shut my eyes and screamed through my snorkel—they heard me on the boat—and lashed out blindly with my speargun.

When I opened my eyes the snake had gone. I felt pretty foolish. But it was a good introduction because it made me respect sea snakes. This is just as well, because we do a lot of filming with them. They're dramatic, like sharks, and there's always a demand in Japan and America for television film.

In the filming we've learned a lot about them. One of our most interesting trips was for *National Geographic* in 1971, at the Swain Reefs about 240 km off the Queensland coast. Ken MacLeish was there from the magazine and a scientist Dr Harold Heatwole. We went out in Ron Isbel's charter boat *Sea Hunt*.

Harold was a herpetologist—snake expert—who had done a lot of field research in the little known area of sea snakes and we learned a great deal about them from him. Ben and Harold even discovered a new species on that trip to add to the other fifty-one varieties already known.

One of the things Dr Heatwole couldn't tell us was what makes sea snakes such grumpy characters at times.

They're the only marine creatures I know that will attack without apparent provocation. Most wild animals will fight if backed into a corner. That's natural. But snakes sometimes seem to look for trouble.

We've had them attack divers over and over, pecking their wetsuits like angry birds. Fortunately they only have short fangs and don't get through the rubber unless it's a very large snake.

104

We had a bad scare with David Krassoff one time. We'd been filming him with a particularly large and aggressive snake. Soon after he got out of the water he complained of headache and exhaustion—the first symptoms of a bite, which is painless in other respects.

We had some anti-venene. But it was a kind developed for a different Malaysian sea snake, *Enhydrina schistosa*, and one that could cause a severe reaction if a bite wasn't present.

The five foot sea snake, *Aipysurus laevis*, swims at Eva Cropp who backpeddles to avoid it.

Eva Cropp taking surface meter reading for a Nikonos camera.

So we put out a call on the two-way radio and set off for shore. After a while, we gave David a urine test and were very relieved to find he was OK. What had happened was that he was involuntarily holding his breath for long periods (he was on SCUBA) when the snake was coiling around him and had given himself a dose of carbon dioxide build-up.'

None of the divers have received a poison bite on the Cropp expeditions. But the possibility is something they have to live with.

Though the sea snake has a comparatively inefficient bite compared with land snakes such as the tiger or taipan, its venom is very potent. The *Enhydrina schistosa*, for instance, has venom ten times as concentrated as a cobra. It is several times more toxic than a tiger, or death adder, though on account of the small mouth and short teeth there is less chance of it getting into a human being's bloodstream.

Nonetheless there are a significant number of deaths in the Indo-Pacific tropics every year—an area extending from the Red Sea and Persian Gulf to the Bay of Bengal, Indonesia, Malaysia, the Philippines, and Vietnam.

Most of the victims are net fishermen bitten while handling nets. Statistics are difficult to get because not only are snakes considered unlucky (which is understandable), but it is also supposed to be bad luck to talk about them.

In Malaya one area of seventeen villages had 144 bites and forty-one deaths (that they would admit to) over a ten-year period. But it is probable that because of superstition the real figures were much higher. In that area, for instance, it was believed that if you are bitten by a sea snake and talk about it, you will certainly be bitten again. Also it is believed that if a pregnant woman hears about a sea snake bite she will die.

The scientists who investigated the villages concluded for these reasons that the bite incidence could be as high as 150 a year.

This would be multiplied many times through the fishing villages of Indo-Pacific regions. Curiously there are no sea snakes in the tropical West Indies, Atlantic, or West African areas.

Symptoms from a bite—a nibbling chewing action which is comparatively painless—may take from five minutes to as long as eight hours to appear. The usual signs are stiffness and aching of the muscles, with paralysis developing in severe cases. Death comes from respiratory failure.

The paralysis is not a rictus—with none of the cramping or agonising twists of rabies or tetanus—but flaccid, completely relaxed. There are stories of victims who heard themselves pronounced dead but could not make the words or movements to protest.

Death may come in several hours or several days. If a victim survives a week, recovery is considered certain. The mortality rate on Malaysian bites is seventeen per cent, with most of the badly bitten victims dying in twelve to twenty-four hours.

Treatment recommended for sea snake bites is similar to that used against the poison of land snakes, with a torniquet applied as soon as possible. The Commonwealth Serum Laboratories in Melbourne have an anti-venene prepared for *Enhydrina schistosa*. This has not yet been tested on *Aipysurus laevis*, the big olive snake of the Barrier Reef and Coral Sea, which is the most aggressive in these regions, or *Microcephalophis gracilis*, or *Astrotia stokesii*, which are also encountered.

Sea snakes eat small fish and marine creatures and have few enemies.

Ben Cropp believes that the confidence snakes show in approaching large and unfamiliar objects (divers) in open water shows that they have not much to fear in their ordinary environment. Experiments he has carried out feeding portions of snake to tame fish show that most reef fish spit out pieces of snake—even disguised—where they will greedily gobble most other food.

'The aggression is something we haven't entirely fathomed', Eva says, 'though it is certainly true that we go to the Swains and the other reefs in June and July at the time when the snakes are mating.

They're particularly bad tempered if disturbed at that time—and I suppose that's easily understood.

They're really very beautiful and sensuous when they're mating. One follows the other through the water, entwining in convolutions so that sometimes you wonder where one snake begins and the other ends . . .

Because they're so short-sighted they sometimes make embarrassing mistakes —with pieces of nylon rope, or the anchor line. Their expression, when they find out they're in love with a piece of prickly nylon or an iron chain is absolutely comical.

We take a few liberties with them making films—catching them by the tail and so on. But by and large we're pretty careful.

Not all of them attack. Perhaps only one in ten at the time when they're most aggressive, and often it's something the diver does which triggers them off.

The Cropps dining on crayfish.

They don't like sudden movements, or to be bumped, and a sure way of making them furious is to kick at them with a flipper.

They're very curious and like to crawl around you and explore you—if you can stand it!

If you can't, the best way to get rid of them is to block their view with a flipper, keeping absolutely still. After a time they get bored and go back to the bottom again.

Kill them? Oh no! I wouldn't kill one, unless it was absolutely necessary to save someone's life. I hate killing. I've never been a spearwoman, and don't like to see fish speared.

I'm much more interested in live animals and creatures. If I could have my wish I guess I'd be a marine biologist. As it is I make films on sea creatures with Ben. That's fun too. Even with sea snakes.'

Eva and Ben Cropp prepare for a dive at Heron Island on the Great Barrier Reef.

The sea snakes go through beautiful courting rites. But because they are short-sighted they sometimes make comic mistakes—like falling in love with a piece of old rope, or the anchor chain. ◄

Eva photographs a one and a half metre olive sea snake in the Coral Sea. ►

A Year of Whales

JOHN HARDING

Thirty-one years old, a pleasant and adventurous soul, he makes marine movies, organises divers' festivals, and gives lectures on the underwater world.

He was a founder and editor of *Fathom* magazine, has been a member of scientific expeditions examining the crown of thorns starfish on the Great Barrier Reef and Pacific islands such as Truk and Guam, and he has made successful lecture tours on the United States circuit. A lot of Harding's film work has centred around sharks. But he regards some of his most memorable experiences as involving whales at a time when he knew very little about them.

It was a quite incredible day. One of those an underwater photographer dreams of, and then has nightmares about later. Mostly about the lost chances. Though I figure in retrospect I was lucky to see the whales at all. In twenty years diving it didn't happen before 1966, my own year of whales, and it hasn't happened since.

It began on the morning of September 1st, 1966. The first day of spring. I was thinking what a beautiful day it was and how we should be out diving when the phone rang. It was Mike Perry, a newspaper friend.

'Hey', he said, barely suppressed excitement in his voice. 'There's a couple of whales down in the Bay here at Balmoral.'

'Uh?' I was not really registering.

'Yes, with a whole flotilla of pleasure boats following them about. They'd make a great news-picture story. Grab your camera and let's go!'

I was slower I must confess. 'It'll probably be gone by the time we get there. Besides the Harbour water's so filthy that you'd never get a picture.'

'We'll never know if we don't try,' said Mike.

I realised I was being negative. 'OK' I said. 'I'll hitch up the boat. We'll launch at Rose Bay ramp.'

I had a 4.6 metre De Havilland aluminium runabout at the time, with twin 40 Evinrudes. It was pretty quick and by the time we got round to Grotto Point we saw the whales were still there.

In fact they weren't going anywhere. They were obviously lost, and worse still, in danger of being run aground or injured by the propellers of the flock of spectator craft which were hounding them. People can be very cruel at times, quite unintentionally. I felt sorry for the huge creatures. One was obviously a mother, the other a calf.

It seemed to me that the baby had just been born, and that the two of them had blundered into the busiest part of Sydney Harbour, perhaps looking for a quiet bay. They had found instead a bedlam of strange shapes and noises that bewildered and confused them. What if the mother abandoned the calf, I thought? It was a bad scene.

Apart from the yachts and motor boats about the place, the whales were close to the track of the Manly ferries and the hydrofoils skating along at 48 km/h raised up on their knife-like fins. They'd chop a whale to pieces. There were also big ocean-going craft passing. It was no place for a mother whale and new baby to be creating a marine traffic hazard.

Pictures being obviously hopeless at that stage in the murky water, we decided to try to get them back to the open sea. We might have a chance of a picture out there and at least we'd be doing the whales a favour.

We had already found that the mother responded to the sound of the outboard motors. If we revved them in neutral just behind her tail she would move directly away with the calf following. By cutting across some boats and yelling at others we managed to get her clear of the melee and anyway most of them had seen enough. Gradually we worked her out into open water. At one time she dived off towards the gasworks at Manly. Another time she headed for Circular Quay.

But in the end we got her outside the Heads, and once she was away from the shallows and the noises the cow seemed much better. She was swimming strongly with more purpose and without making the nervous darts to left or right of earlier on.

The calf always stayed just above her back, a light-coloured patch which showed us which way the mother was heading and no doubt the reason why she never dived deeply.

We found out later they were 'right whales', once one of the world's commonest species, and now one of the rarest. The old whalers called them 'right' whales because they were easy to harpoon and floated once killed—the right whale to catch.

They were baleen whales with mouths full of huge brushes for straining krill, shrimps, and plankton. Once they swam in thousands off the Australian coast. But they were hunted so hard early in the 1800s that by 1850 they were already scarce. They were declared protected in 1929. But many marine zoologists consider that this was much too late to save the species. One more creature on the extinction list, and another black mark against the commercial greed of the human race.

At any rate there we were off Sydney Heads with a couple of the last of the 'right' whales.

The cow whale breached black and enormous just ahead of our boat.

She spouted with a whistling sigh, and a feather of steam and water rose vertically from her blow-hole and puffed away on the wind. A pale patch just below the surface showed where the calf was keeping station next to her.

The moment for a dive had come. Heart pounding, I slung the camera round my neck by its strap and pulled down my mask.

'Drop me just ahead', I said, trying to keep the tremor out of my voice. 'And drive her past me!'

As I rolled over the rail with a splash I was scared. 'This is it, Harding.'

The diver with me had refused point blank to go in. I didn't blame him.

We had no idea how the whale would behave, except that, predictably, she would be more likely to be aggressive because of the calf with her. I knew toothed whales like the sperm whale had killed men in whaling days and that one photographer had lost his life in the Atlantic through taking a close-up too close.

What did baleen whales do?

There was no use worrying about it—I'd find out soon enough. And so in I went, hitting the water hard from the moving boat. It was cold and none too clear. The colour of the sea was dark green from the seventy metre depth below me. Divers like to be able to see bottom, and the yawning abyss below did nothing to steady my nerves.

The boat revved down-wind and I swivelled around looking for the whale. Suddenly she was there. The most enormous, terrifying yet beautiful thing I have ever seen under water.

She was black, and silent, moving with powerful strokes of her tail. And from the small portion of her back and head we had seen above water we could never have imagined the breadth and girth of her. I had swum with a whale shark of fourteen metres but it would have been pilot fish size alongside this monster.

I looked in the viewfinder of the camera, trying to focus as she surged down on me, and when I saw her the fear and admiration were forgotten in frustration and disappointment.

Only a cameraman could really understand. But the whale was black, and

The strip of her back on the surface we saw from the boat gave no indication of the incredible bulk below.

John Harding.

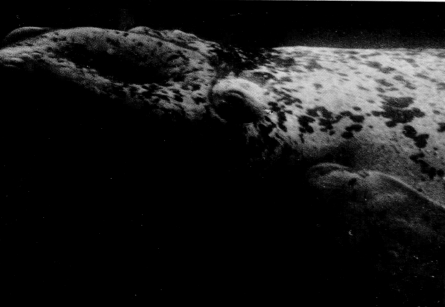

Close-up of the baby's head. Strange how a thing five and a half metres long and a couple of tonnes in weight can seem so little and helpless. ◄

We managed to get close enough to touch the calf's tail. ►

merged into the dark background in perfect harmony. Perfect for her natural camouflage. But so hopeless for photography I could have wept in my mask. Gone were the visions of the picture of the year! All I looked like getting was a great black blank.

The problem was that the Rollei had a telephoto effect. This meant that to get the whole whale, or even a recognisable part of her, in frame I would have had to stand off a long way. And then in the dirty water I couldn't see her at all!

As a final blow the only film I'd been able to grab that morning was a 16 ASA black-and-white. So slow as to be almost useless under water.

With a modern Nikonos and fish-eye lens, of course, or a Nikon-F in a housing with a 20 or 24 mm wide-angle and corrected part, and colour film—all the 1974 gear—I could have got some great pictures. But this was back in 1966 and out there with my Rollei it was a bit like trying to photograph a battleship in a fog from five metres away. You could get one eye of the whale in (funny how small they are), but none of the majesty and breath-taking effect of the total dimension.

I was cursing none too softly on the surface, saying vile things to the seagulls, when the calf showed up and I switched from the depth of despondency to something approaching delight. We'd get some pictures after all!

It was light-coloured and showed well against the dark background, and it was small enough—if you call five and a half metres and two tonnes 'small'—to get a reasonable amount of it in frame. I took some good shots of its head and funny little puckered mouth as it went past.

Though they seemed to be moving slowly, in fact the whales finned through the ocean at a very respectable rate, and I winded myself trying to keep up. But I blasted off the rest of my roll of twelve pictures and felt much better by the last frame.

I was still excited by that first never-to-be-forgotten sight of the cow whale appearing in front of me out of the gloom like a train coming out of a tunnel. And she hadn't eaten me or walloped me with her tail either, which was nice.

I clambered into the boat to re-load the camera, gave Mike the OK sign, and persuaded the other diver to come in and give some size comparison in the pictures.

I didn't blame him for his earlier refusal. I was scared myself and he wasn't getting any of the glory. But seeing that I had survived he agreed to come in the second time.

Baby sperm-whale at North Narrabeen. We did everything we could to save it, and the whale could easily have got back into deep water.

Pilot-whales; a rare sight for a diver. The pod disappeared into the blue and that was the last we saw of them.

▲

heads. The spray and noise were unbelievable. I remember thinking what a mess it would make if it hit you. Then we fled unashamedly, hauling ourselves over the edge of the boat as Mike Perry gunned the motors and whisked us out of there.

The cow turned away with a look of satisfaction, and the last we saw of them they were continuing on their northward path, rolling, and blowing and eating up the kilometres. It was nice to feel that we'd done something to help.

It turned out to be a year of whales. Not long after, a young sperm whale was stranded in the surf at North Narrabeen. That was a sad story.

The whale could easily have got back into deep water. But it seemed determined to strand itself and die, resisting all efforts to get it off the shallows. When we tried to roll it over it braced its tail to prevent us. Pulling with a rope and launch was no good either. It just didn't want to live. Whale suicides are not uncommon, and are one of the things which puzzle scientists. This was one of them.

Next day it was dead, and the local council dug a whale-sized hole with a bulldozer and buried it.

My third encounter with whales was in September 1967—exactly a year after the 'right' whales. It was at a reef sixteen kilometres east of Lizard Island off the Great Barrier Reef.

I was with Ron and Valerie Taylor on a Belgian scientific expedition. About 9.30 a.m. I was on deck and said to Val, 'Look at those porpoises!' A minute or two later I realised that the creatures leaping out of the water weren't porpoises at all. They had blunt bottle heads and were much bigger—five to eight metres.

'Pilot whales! Quick, grab a camera!'

The crew dropped us from a rubber dinghy and we caught up with the pilot whales near a shallow reef. I saw one dart forward and grab a two kilo trevally. It grabbed it like a dog and I saw bubbles go up as the fish's air bladder broke. Then it swallowed it in a gulp.

The pilot whales let us get within four metres of them. But they sheered off nervously if we got closer. Gradually they worked into deeper water, and left us for the open sea.

That was my year with the cetaceans—the whales, large and small. As it turned out I didn't win fame or fortune as I'd hoped. But looking back the money doesn't really count. They were extraordinary experiences, and show what an enormous part luck plays in underwater photography.

I managed to get some pictures of him hanging on to the calf's tail and touched the mother's tail myself. Even though it was enormous and my touch was light, she felt it and gave an irritated thump with her flukes.

I got some good shots of the calf's head, and then the mother's patience wore thin. She had had a bad afternoon bottled up among the boats in the Harbour, and now we were buzzing around her nose like a pair of submarine gadflies, annoying the hell out of her and disturbing the calf.

Just as I clicked the last shot she rounded on us, and away to the left I saw the huge mouth opening like a garage door.

'Look out!' I shouted on the surface, back-pedalling, and then added rather unnecessarily, 'let's get out of here!'

At that moment she lifted her huge tail up in the air. I watched it for a moment mesmerised. Then it came down THWACK!!! a metre from our

The First *Zuytdorp* Dive

MAX CRAMER

The Zeeland ship *Zuytdorp* was one of the biggest vessels in the Dutch East India Company and a veteran of two previous Indies voyages when she left Holland in July 1711, with a smaller vessel, the *Belvliet*.

They carried a cargo of silver. Money from the Middelburgh mint, brand new and shining and each piece dated 1711. The *Zuytdorp* carried at least 250,000 guilders worth and she may have had as much as 500,000 guilders in silver in the iron-bound chests chained to the deck below the captain's cabin.

Rich as they were, the ships had a nightmare voyage. The *Zuytdorp* reached the Cape of Good Hope in March 1712 with 112 of her 286 crew dead and twenty-two carried ashore to hospital. This at only the half-way mark of the voyage. The little *Belvliet* lost sixty men (including her skipper Dirk Blauw) from a complement of sixty-four. When she finally reached Batavia in the East Indies the *Belvliet* had only four of the fifty-eight soldiers who had marched aboard in Holland in their fine uniforms still alive.

How the *Zuytdorp* was wrecked or what the miserable aftermath was for the men who scrambled ashore on hostile red cliffs no one knows. We can only conjecture. It was a wretched place to die. . . .

In modern times the shore wreckage was located as early as 1927, but consistently rough seas at the site made it a difficult place to dive. Though a number of expeditions went to the remote spot in isolated sheep station country from the 1950s onwards, none of them was able to find a break in the swells which rolled thundering in from the Indian Ocean. The wreck site kept its secrets—until May 11th, 1964.

Going wreck diving on a camel might seem a crazy notion. But there were times on our expedition to the 1712 *Zuytdorp* in 1964 when we would gladly have traded in our Willys jeep for a couple of well-seasoned camels.

I reckon they would have tackled the territory along the *Zuytdorp* cliffs and the inland track more efficiently, and we couldn't have been more uncomfortable than we already were, bouncing and sliding from one side of the jeep utility tray to the other. Lead belts, kitbags, and all our heavy gear banging beside us. And under us, and on top of us . . .

Not that the jeep couldn't take it. The vehicle straddled the sandhills, the boulders and the limestone outcrops without missing a beat. The problem was human frailty. Ten years later I still remember the bruises.

No one who hasn't seen it can imagine what the *Zuytdorp* track was like. It was only sixty-four kilometres. But it took us most of the night, and on the back of that hardwood tray the time fairly lingered as we crawled from rock to rock and sandhill to sandhill through the hours of darkness.

It was a track used by pack horses and—yes, camels—in the old days. The old route to Shark Bay, long since abandoned. Men died of thirst out there, once, and got lost and went mad, tearing off their clothes and going in smaller and smaller circles in the desolation. I can understand it. And seeing the wild, desolate, and hostile country I felt sorry for the Dutch sailors who probably perished there too when their ship was wrecked in the winter of 1712.

Why did we follow the madman's track?

Our fundamental objective was to make the first dive on the 1712 *Zuytdorp*. They say all wreck divers are a little crazy, and in the eyes of many people our aim in attempting to swim on the *Zuytdorp*—the wreck everyone said was impossible—wasn't just a mild case of mania. It was madness of the stark, staring kind.

We thought differently, of course. We figured we had the whole thing worked out to a reasonable and rational proposition, and taking the inland track was a considered part of the plan.

Though there were a lot of mysteries about the wreck—what happened to the men who got off her, for instance—there was no mystery about why no one had been able to dive on her.

The ship lies under the projecting ledges of a sea-swept reef at the foot of beetling cliffs—smashed in ten thousand pieces among the rocks and blowholes.

Most days of the year the swell from the Indian Ocean breaks heavily across the reef. The deep water ends less than ninety metres from shore and the swells come in steep and high straight off the open sea. They break with a force that sends the spray flying hundreds of metres high in the air from the whistling blowholes in the reef.

At one point where the cliffs rise to 300 m, a place the old natives called 'Womeranjie', the spray comes over the top in a fine drizzle on a sou'west wind. You can hear the waves breaking in the cliff caves from kilometres inland on a still night.

A lot of divers—good men too—went there to try to dive on the wreck before 1964. They looked at the white seething foam, and the suck-back of the

A reconstruction of the *Zuytdorp*.

surge over black rocks studded with razor-sharp oyster shells. Then they shook their heads, and turned around and went home again without getting their gear wet.

The force of the waves was just too tremendous. If a man got in there, there was no way he could get out again without being either sucked up into the blowhole system or shredded on the oyster rocks. Even if he did get in he would be blind in the foam and would see nothing but a white crackling curtain of bubbles before he cracked his skull on some rock or other.

But old-timers told us that there were occasional days, freak days, when the swell dropped and there was a brief calm along the cliffs. Days when they could pull their snapper-fishing dinghies alongside and step out on to the rocks.

These days came once a year, or perhaps even only once in two or three years. Usually the calm lasted only a few hours. But if you were there on one of those once-a-year days a dive would be possible.

This was where our great advantage came in, living at Geraldton. Where divers from Perth, 800 km south, couldn't afford the time to dally indefinitely on the cliff top hoping for the kind of day which came once a year, we could watch and wait at home.

Geraldton is only 241 km south of the wreck, and we figured that we might be able to make a dash and get there on a calm before the weather broke.

But on our part of the coast really flat calms usually only come when a cyclone is moving south, or before a big storm. There is no anchorage closer to the wreck than the Murchison River, sixty-four kilometres south, which shuts out quickly in bad weather. Even Geraldton has surf breaking right across the harbour in a big blow. The idea of taking a boat up the coast was a doubtful proposition.

We settled for the land trip, jolts, bruises, and all. You can tell from this that we weren't considering setting ourselves up as heroes. There's a saying that there are old divers and bold divers, but no old bold divers. And my ambition was, and is, ultimately, to be an old, old diver. To make sure the thing was feasible we made one reconnaissance trip. The surf was high, but we figured that in the right circumstances a dive could be made.

There was myself, and my brother Graham, and Tom Brady as divers, as well as Tom Muir, who owned the jeep, and Alf Morgan, a rabbit trapper who was our guide. On later trips Neil McLaughlan and Gordon Hancock came along.

There were several false alarms, and when the day finally came we could hardly believe it. We watched all morning waiting for those little dark clouds on the horizon, a breath of wind out of the north, or some other sign that the weather was going to break. But it stayed just perfect, and by lunchtime we were well on our way. It was 10th May, 1964.

The vehicle had been thoroughly checked out in Tom Brady's garage. We'd organised our businesses and our wives, and fixed all the trying little things that somehow crop up at the last minute when you want to be off in a hurry.

The first 100 km on a bitumen highway were fine. The next ninety on the gravel road into Murchison River were rougher. But it was when we crossed the river at the ford that we got into the true bush terrain.

All the time we were thinking about the *Zuytdorp*. No one really knew what would be at the foot of the cliffs. We didn't even know how deep it would be.

The blowholes worried us. Would be we sucked into some black sinister gap under the reef and jammed there . . .? Or even fired out like a cork out of a champagne bottle? Or just ripped to pieces on the razor-sharp rock oyster shells?

To take our minds off the blowholes we thought about the silver. The *Zuytdorp* was carrying chests of it. More than 250,000 guilders worth. We knew that coins were flung up on the reef in heavy weather, seeming to indicate that there must be a stack of them loose in the water. A lot of old Dutch relics had been found on the cliffs above and the bluffs beyond, showing that many of the crew must have gone ashore.

Tom Pepper, a Murchison House Station boundary rider, was the first to find the wreck. He was tracking down a dingo that had been killing sheep in April 1927 when he saw a way down the cliff. He took out a fishing line from his saddle-bag and went down to try for some snapper. On the rocks he saw some curious things. Green discs, and a lot of strange woodwork. One piece was carved, with the figure of a woman with a lion on her breast. The discs turned out to be coins with the inscription ZEELANDIA and the date 1711 on them. And there were other things, including broken bottles, belt buckles, and some heavy brass objects which later turned out to be cannon breech blocks.

He wasn't greatly pleased at the time. Tom was a wonderful bushman able to track a dingo on horseback, and a crack shot. But he was something of a recluse, as natural bushmen often are, preferring the hermit life. He didn't want the police and all kinds of strangers swarming out from town over his part of the world. At first he said nothing about the find, except to his wife Lurlie and immediate family.

But after they carried the woman-carving back on a packhorse the word got out. A message was sent from officialdom down south that he was to take everything in to the police station at Northampton and hand it over. Especially the 'figurehead' as the carving came to be called (though it was actually a piece from the stern of the vessel).

'I'll be damned if I will', Tom said with spirit. And he added that he would toss the whole lot back in the sea if they tried to come and get it. 'Then they can swim for it.' Divers who came in succeeding years appreciated the joke behind that remark.

Some newspaper people and police came in 1939, but Tom was conveniently 'away' looking for stray sheep when they came and they had to deal with Mrs Pepper. After that people left Tom alone.

Not much happened until after the war in the 1950s, when a geologist called Philip Playford heard the story and sought Tom out at Shark Bay where he was the overseer on Tamala Station. Tom told Playford a lot of things he hadn't told anyone else, and after visiting the wreck site the geologist organised two expeditions in company with West Australian Newspapers in 1954 and 1958. They found more coins on the reef and a lot of unmistakable signs that the *Zuytdorp*'s crew had got ashore. But they didn't solve any mysteries and though divers went on both expeditions, the surf never dropped to anywhere near a level possible for diving.

The newspaper stories generated a lot of interest, and many other divers went to the site, but with similar lack of success. The most important thing was that Phil Playford managed to get a lot of research information from Holland. Among other things he found that the 1711 coin was a consignment sent aboard the long-missing *Zuytdorp*, and this positively identified the ship.

And so we jolted along the track in May 1964 at the non-express speed of eight kilometres-an-hour, with our imaginations fully active.

After Giji outcamp, the track—now simply two tyre ruts in the bush—got worse and sometimes disappeared altogether where flocks of travelling sheep had obliterated it. Several times we had to get out and hunt around in the

The freak day on which we dived; the best day in three years.▼

The familiar shape of old Dutch cannon. ▲

Zuytdorp coins; Dubbele Stuiver and Schellingen next to five cent piece. Coins from Middelburgh mint dated 1711 identified the wreck. ▼

darkness with torches to find it. We began to run into sandhill-stretches where we had to let the tyres down to get traction. Invariably these would be followed by areas of limestone outcrops where we had to pump the tyres up to avoid damaging them.

Eventually, early in the morning, we got close to the wreck. It had taken us 17 hours to travel the 241 km. The first 160 km were covered in two hours, the last eleven kilometres into the wreck site through limestone and ti-tree thickets also took two hours.

It was 5 a.m. when we reached the cliffs. Still an hour to winter daylight, and of course none of us had slept that night. We stretched stiff legs and looked over the cliff, straining eyes in the darkness. The air was still leaden calm. There was no sound of surf. So we crossed our fingers and hoped, and for an hour we slept in the vehicle.

At 6 a.m. we were up and moving down to the water's edge with our gear. In the early morning light we could see that the surf was still low. Good enough to go in, we reckoned, though a medium wave swept in once in a while.

It is impossible to describe the excitement of that moment. We had already experienced something of it with the *Batavia* off the Abrolhos in 1963. But there had been more build up to this dive—more worry, anticipation and apprehension, because of the fearsome reputation of the place, and because of the persistent rumours that other divers planned a similar expedition. We badly wanted to be first and now it was within our reach.

Trying to keep reasonably calm, I got my gear on. Tom Brady and my brother Graham at that time had little diving experience and I did my best to instruct them in the best way to get into the surf—and out.

As soon as I got clear of the foam of the waves I started to see the familiar signs of shipwreck. Straight lines and regular forms showed on the bottom, and my heart beat faster as I sighted one cannon then another. Then there was a bronze cannon worn away by sand so that it looked as though half the barrel had been cut away lengthwise so it looked like one of those cutaway models of car engines you see with the pistons exposed.

At the south end of the wreck were a couple of large anchors showing that—as we'd always believed—the *Zuytdorp* had lain right alongside the rock before the waves beat her to pieces.

Towards the reef the water was still white with foam. A very significant area we were to find out later. But on that day the other two weren't particularly confident swimmers and we didn't venture into the area of surge and swirl.

A row of regular forms caught my eye, and diving down I found that there were layers of ingots, some stacked in regular piles, other spilled out across the sea-bed. On a thought that they might be silver, I chipped off a sliver with my diving knife. But it was just lead.

We were free-diving, and after the long night's drive and the excitement, plus the surge and swirl even on this calm day, were beginning to get pretty tired when I spotted some green shapes in a pothole. Green on a wreck means either copper, brass, or silver, any of which are likely to be interesting. Down I went and found what at first looked for all the world like modern navy four-inch shell cases.

I grabbed one and realised with the weight of it that it was nothing to do with HMAS *Sydney* or any of the wartime ships lost in the area. It was a small bronze cannon a little over half a metre long, worn by sea and sand and that thundering daily surf since 1712. But it was beautiful to our eyes as wreck hunters.

We salvaged all three, dragging them to the rocks with difficulty because we were by now well and truly tired. After we'd passed them up to Tom Muir and Alf Morgan and dragged ourselves out of the surf we sat there tired but happy. As we sat the weather changed. The sea, which had been still and calm, broke into a short chop with long swell and the wind began to blow out of the north. The calm was over.

On that trip we did not find the silver—a solid bank of gleaming coin edge on edge three metres long and half a metre high under a ledge. It was in the white foam under the blowhole point, and the find of the 'schellinger' and 'dubbele stuivers' with their 1711 dates, the ducatons and pieces-of-eight was to wait for a later trip by Tom Brady, Gordon Hancock and Neil McLaughlan. Silver which lies there yet. . . .

But in May 1964 we had achieved our objective. We had been the first men to dive on the *Zuytdorp* wreck, and that afternoon as our vehicle crawled back along the *Zuytdorp* track the bumps and bruises were nothing compared with our elation and sense of achievement.

Now ten years after it happened people sometimes ask me 'What did it prove?'

The only answer I can give is: 'We were the first.'

The Invisible Invaders

NEVILLE COLEMAN

Each summer when the onshore winds blow harsh and hot in the north and the blood-warm waters off the creeks and beaches become thick as soup with sediment, an invisible invader comes in on the tide.

Anywhere from Broome on the Western Australian coast round to Queensland and occasionally as far south as Moreton Bay and the Gold Coast, box jellyfish drift in the murky summer shallows trailing long stinging tendrils behind their opaque translucent bodies.

Little is known about them.

How they breed, where they come from and where they go to, are matters still open to scientific question.

What IS positively known is that in northern areas in past summers, a number of Australians have died agonising deaths from the stings of the box jellyfish—the inappropriate name of the sea wasp.

For no wasp ever stung as agonisingly or lethally as these coelanterates which can, in the right (or wrong) combination of circumstances, kill a healthy man or child in two minutes—as long as it takes to read the introduction to this story.

It is typical of Neville Coleman, a diving naturalist with the true spirit of inquiry, that he allowed a sea wasp to sting him.

The Colemans, Neville and Barbara, arrived in Darwin in the warm steaming mid-summer days of the sea wasp season. The time of the cubomedusas.

At the beach they found a sign which read:

WARNING
Sea Wasps Are Deadly
In these Waters Between
October and May

In front of the sign a number of people were swimming although the sea wasp season was well advanced. To Neville Coleman this was entirely satisfactory.

He and his wife had come around Australia from Sydney, diving in the cold southern waters of Victoria and South Australia, crossing the border into Western Australia, where 6 500 kilometres of coastline offered all the changes of temperature and living creatures a diving naturalist could hope for.

His original plan was to dive every 160 kilometres. In practice it did not work out this way due to problems of pure geography which occasionally defeated their four-wheel drive vehicle. Or sometimes more practical matters of fuel and food supplies which were baffling and frustrating to a purist natural historian.

Nevertheless he achieved a great deal and after three years of travel and recording and collecting specimens of sub-tidal marine life, he arrived in Darwin quite intentionally at the right time for sea wasps—the deadly box jellyfish. Coleman hoped to find sea wasps in the water, to observe them in their natural habitat, and if possible to photograph them—though he was aware that in the dirty-water conditions in which they are found this would be difficult.

He also hoped to talk to people who had been stung by the creatures, and he reasoned that since he would be there at the right time of year he might be lucky enough to be around when someone got stung—hopefully not fatally so that they could talk about it.

All these things happened, but not before he had gone through one of the periods of frustration so familiar to naturalists and divers. He waded around day after day, camera slung around his neck, sloshing waist deep in the bath-warm waters of Darwin Harbour hoping to run into a sea wasp. Since he did not want to make it the kind of encounter which would impair his ability to make scientific records he was wearing a wetsuit and jeans. And it was hot. Stifling, sweating, stickily hot.

On the shore his wife Barbara walked too, only slightly less hot, and carrying the antidote. This was alcohol, a large plastic container of methylated spirits, because if no one else got stung Neville Coleman was determined to try the cubomedusa himself, in controlled circumstances.

One of the things which is reliably known about the box jellies is that alcohol or meths dry up the stinging tentacles and neutralise the poison out of the neomycites injected into the skin by the tentacles.

A great deal else remains unknown.

Though sea wasp deaths and injuries must have occurred for centuries among the Aborigines (and at Melville Island they have a traditional name for it, 'Irukandji') most of our own knowledge dates from as late as the 1950s. It was only then that the first formal medical identification was made of the box jellyfish by Dr Flecker following a fatality in northern Queensland.

Before this there had certainly been deaths. In 1884, for instance, a seaman named John Kelly at Ross Creek near Townsville heard an eleven-year-old boy give a terrible scream near his house.

'He was in no more than three feet of water', said Kelly. 'I heard him scream, and saw him slapping at his legs. Then he fell down. I had it in my mind he'd cut his foot on a bottle, and I ran across. He was already dead when I picked him up, and he was covered with the slime and tendrils like transparent string clinging to him. When I picked him up I was stung myself, and had to get treatment from Dr Ridgeley . . .'

Typical among other cases cited in Cleland and Southcott's book *Injuries to Man from Marine Invertebrates in the Australian Region* were:

A man of thirty-six at Proserpine, in 1923, dived into the water and was stung on the left arm and ankle. His widow said that he came running out of the sea crying, 'I'm stung!' and then collapsed and died. There were deep purple marks on his arm and ankle.

An Italian cane worker, about twenty-eight years old, bathing at Googarra, near Tully, North Queensland, in 1934 leaped out of the water crying something in Italian. He reached the beach and threw himself on the beach rubbing sand on his legs in agony. Within minutes he had lapsed into unconsciousness and died. He too had the significant weals, like whip-marks around his legs.

A thirteen-year-old girl, in 1941, at Townsville, was swimming with friends off the rocks near the basin swimming enclosure. She said she had been stung and a man saw tentacles hanging from her chest and arms. 'I applied wet sand and after five minutes saw the girl's eyes throw back and she began to froth at the mouth . . . I tried to open her hand in which she had sand, but could not, so she must have been in pain . . .'

The list goes on. There are nearly forty recorded fatal cases in Australia and New Guinea, and many stings ranging from near-fatal to relatively mild. Some people who recovered from bad stings have scars for life—a typical recessed livid mark on the skin.

It goes almost without saying that many fatalities, in early pioneering days, and many less severe stings, must have gone unrecorded altogether.

One of the strange features of sea wasp history is that people so long regarded the creature responsible as the Portuguese man-o-war or blue-bottle. This is the jellyfish with the conspicuous blue float, the familiar *Physalia utriculus*, so frequently washed up in summer months.

Physalia can give a bad sting, as anyone knows who has had its long trailing blue tentacles wrap around them like a red-hot wire while surfing but it was Dr Flecker, working on stinging coelanterates early in the 1950s, who noticed a number of factors which didn't add up. One was that while jellyfish deaths were a recognised occurrence in the north there was none south of Brisbane. Yet the same Portuguese man-o-war believed to be responsible was found in numbers off Sydney beaches as well as in Victoria, South Australia, and Western Australia. Though they occasionally put people in hospital, jellyfish did not kill anyone south of the Tropic of Capricorn. Could there be another species as yet unidentified? Flecker believed there was and had his theory confirmed when a commonsense policeman had the sea netted after a north Queensland death to get evidence for the Coroner's Inquiry. Some odd-shaped creatures were caught in the nets. They were bell-shaped transparent jellyfish up to 203 mm across, trailing very strong tentacles four and a half to six metres long similar to those described in incidents in the past.

Dr Flecker examined these cubomedusas and found that they had an intensely potent venom, which readily and rapidly killed laboratory rats and mice. They were identified as the mystery killer of the north—the sea wasp. The particular species was named *Chironex fleckeri*, and the enemy was at last identified.

Subsequently it was found that there were two fatal box (because of the four square lower corners of the body) jellyfish in the north. The first, and probably most potent, was *Chironex fleckeri*, named in honour of the man who identified them. The next to be identified was *Chiropsalmus quadrigatus*.

Either can kill. But neither are by any means always fatal. The severity of the sting varies with unknown factors in the creature itself—the size of the beast, its sexual state, health, and so on. The area of the victim stung is also important. Many of the fatalities have been caused by people diving into the jellyfish and wrapping it around their head, shoulders and chest. It may be also that some people are more or less resistant than others in the same way that some may be barely affected by a bee sting, others may swell badly, and some people particularly allergic may in extreme cases have to be hospitalised.

Children are generally more susceptible than adults, though cases have been recorded of strong men stung only around the lower legs and still dying a short time later.

The similar features in the fatal occurrences have been the agonising pain, with the victims lapsing quickly into shock and unconsciousness, together with

the fact that the 'attacks' all took place close to shore during warm summer months.

In fact they are not attacks in the true sense of aggression or hunting. As so often happens in the animal world, it is simply an instance of a creature operating its defensive mechanisms when a human being unintentionally threatens or blunders into it.

A major problem, as Neville Coleman was to find, is that the transparent sea wasps, with tentacles trailing up to six metres behind them, are next to invisible in murky northern waters.

'At Darwin I tried for days to find them', he said. 'Finally it just happened.

'I was wading disconsolately about below the warning sign when this lady came in swimming. She was the cook at the Aboriginal hostel, and she just ploughed in.

'I pointed at the warning sign and said, "Aren't you worried about the sea wasps?"

'"Not on your life", she said. "I've been swimming here for years!"

'Next thing she dived, almost at my feet and came up screaming with a sea wasp clinging to her left arm and shoulder.

'I grabbed her and whizzed her into the beach, and Barbara got the methylated spirits to her quickly. It was amazing how rapidly it took the pain away. She was a tough old bird and it must have really hurt her to make her yell like that.

'Of course a crowd gathered, and it didn't help a bit that a couple of insensitive idiots told her, quite seriously, that she was likely to be dead in a few minutes.

'The metho negated the poison pods. The tentacles of a large sea wasp are lined with dark mauve rings. These house thousands of minute poison pods, each with a miniature harpoon in a coiled spring which uncoils in a rotating movement on contact with flesh or other chemical stimulant. Each harpoon shoots in a squirt of poison. The more you struggle the more coils and syringe nematocysts you activate.

'That's why the very worst thing you can do is rub sand on them. It makes you shudder when you read the fatality stories—the people trying to help were really achieving the opposite result.

'The best thing is to try to lift the tentacle with a knife or stick. Then flush the area with alcohol or meths.

'I kept the specimen which stung our Darwin lady, callous though it may have seemed. Despite my concern for her, I wasn't going to let go of the only *Chironex fleckeri* I'd caught up with up to that time!

'After the excitement was over I decided to try a controlled experiment and let it sting me. Barbara wasn't too keen on the idea. But she was even less enthusiastic when I suggested as an alternative we let it sting her.

'I put a piece of tentacle gingerly on my arm to start with. It stung, but it was bearable, though it made a spectacular red weal.

' "Hang it", I thought. "I'll take a risk!" And I put the whole lot on my foot. They certainly stung. Hard enough to bring tears to my eyes almost past the point of control. But I could stand it—just. Next day the weals were practically gone. Obviously it was a very light sting and in this sense I guess it was disappointing.

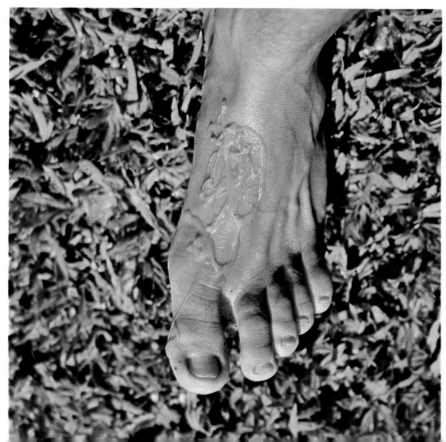

Barbara Coleman displays the deadly spines of the stonefish. ▲

This photo clearly shows what a hazard the venomous stonefish is, with its unsurpassed camouflage. ►

'It may have been that the *Chironex* had used up all its nematocysts on the lady. It's noteworthy in this regard that in fatal cases rescuers have often also been stung, but never as badly as the victims.

'I've had a much worse jolt from a stinging swimming anemone at Dampier in Western Australia. That really knocked me out.

'And the most dangerous thing that happened on the whole trip was a stonefish at Shark Bay. I had him on a table—a horrid, fat warty beast he was—trying to find out how the poison glands worked. I found out all right!

'The glands are activated when the skin on the spikes is pressed down (like when you tread on them!) I remembered when a fellow was hit in North Queensland. He was on a prawning boat and the spine went through his boot. They called for an ambulance over the two-way radio, and in the background over the skipper's voice, you could hear this fellow screaming. It was an unearthly sound. One that sent shivers up your spine.

'It was too far to a port so they simply beached the boat. Ran it aground so they could get him to an ambulance quicker.

'I was thinking of him as I started checking out this stonefish on the table, being wary of any sudden flip of a tail. I'd heard stories of a dried head, nailed to a wall for months falling down and stinging someone. That's how potent the venom is.

'At any rate I depressed the skin on one—only one—spine out of the thirteen, and to my horror a jet of pure venom shot straight at my face. That stuff in your eye could be as bad as in an open wound. The eye is less than two and a half centimetres from the brain.

'Could it kill you? Blind you? I don't know. Luckily it missed my eyes. Instead it hit me on top of the head, and simply gave me a hell of a fright.

'It was a lesson learned. I'm doubly cautious about handling stonefish now.

'Would I prefer to be stung by a stonefish or sea wasp? Hardly a fair question. I think I'd prefer a sea wasp because I know how to defuse the tentacles and stop the venom quickly. But my answer—scientific curiosity satisfied I suppose—would be neither.

'They have a number of things in common. Both have a venom agonising and destructive to humans. Yet both are essentially defensive creatures. They don't attack, and their encounters with humans are accidental from both sides. I guess that's the tragedy of it.'

126